Skybound

Skybound

Roger Jones

Bass Clef Books
Cecilia, KY

First Edition

ISBN

979-8-9898478-7-7

$25.00

Cover art
and interior photographs

Libby Falk Jones

Bass Clef Books is an imprint of MARZEK Publishing
Mick Kennedy publisher

Printed and distributed by
Kindle Direct Publishing

Acknowledgments

I'm grateful for family and flying people for supporting me in my sky journey. Special thanks go to Joe Sanchez, who was an encouraging and knowledgeable presence in all aspects of Cessna 150 lore and in early days of my ownership of the Silent. To Joachim Schneibel, long-time soaring instructor based in Knoxville, TN, and the previous owner of the Silent, who did all he could to make my ownership practical and pleasant. And to my wife, Libby Falk Jones, who made everything possible.

Thanks too to faculty and students of Bluegrass Writers Studio at Eastern Kentucky University for their reading of early versions of some of the chapters of this memoir, and to Richard Taylor, Bob Johnson and Don Ingraham for their words about the book. Thanks as well to Mick Kennedy for his design of the book and cover.

Thanks to the editors of *Soaring* magazine, October 2009, in which earlier versions of parts of Chapters 3 and 5 appeared.

Table of Contents

The Perfect Flight

It's a perfect July day in 2016 in central Kentucky: 75 degrees, light winds and clear skies. Despite the beauty of this Sunday morning, I am nervous when I get out of bed. I am going flying. But more is at stake than the single flight. "Did you run your checklist?" my wife, Libby, asks as we head out the back door to the van in the driveway. I suppress a bubble of irritation. Of course I ran my "go flying" checklist: parachute, headset, white bucket hat, dark glasses, wallet, watch, water. I have been flying for almost 20 years now. I know how to prepare for a flight. Still, I appreciate Lib's intention. She knows I'm nervous; and she knows it's easy to forget things—even a whole checklist—when one is nervous.

The airplane I am to fly is a glider, a high-performance glider with a retractable engine, a self-launching sailplane. It's nine years old, made by Alisport SRL, an Italian manufacturer of fiberglass-and-carbon-fiber sailplanes and carbon-fiber propellers. The plane was custom-made (all new sailplanes are custom orders these days) for an Arizona owner, who sold it to a pilot in Knoxville, Tennessee, from whom I bought it three years ago.

Sailplanes are the most efficient aircraft human beings have ever devised, with their slender, tadpole-shaped fuselages and long, long wings. To sit in this one, I recline almost prone. With the airplane balanced on a single wheel under me, I am barely a foot off the ground. Over my head an optically perfect plexiglass canopy stretches from my feet to the crown of my head. It is designed to disappear from consciousness altogether in flight, like well-worn spectacles.

I have a private pilot's license and ratings for aerotowed and self-launching sailplanes, but this self-launching sailplane has more capabilities than the other pure gliders I have flown. In order to be qualified to fly it—at least as far as the FAA and the insurance company are concerned—I had to journey to Memphis to take instruction with the only pilot in the east who instructs in such a sailplane. Then I had to spend a day in Tullahoma, Tennessee, where the North American distributor for Alisport went with me over the sailplane's every system and construction detail.

Before I could fly the glider much, though, it was beset by engine problems. I used the time it was down to grow fluent in assembling and disassembling the sailplane out of and back into its specialized trailer. During the intervals when the engine permitted it, I worked on my taxiing. Long glider wings require more-than-careful navigation on the ground. I taxied around the ramps, taxiways, and runways of my home airfield in Richmond, Kentucky and the bigger, longer-runwayed facility at London, Kentucky, where I have kept the glider over the last year.

Sorting out the sailplane's engine issues has taken two years. They were long years. The sorting out has taken the combined insights of a triumvirate of experts—a specialist aircraft mechanic from Knoxville, the North-American distributor in Tullahoma, and the parts manager at Alisport in Italy. It has been an arduous process of fits and starts, with much exchange of cell phone photographs. The engine is performing impeccably now, though, and today will be the first day since it has been healthy that I will have the Silent actually in the air. What is making me nervous, though, is not so much the prospect of flying it, but rather a long talk about the glider Lib and I had over the winter. This glider, if it works out, would be the culmination of 60 years of my yearning to fly, 60 years of wanting to soar like a travelling raptor, high and away. This yearning is truly life-long. But now, after a decade of flying pure sailplanes, hang gliders, and power planes, I know that this glider has the capability to fulfill my yearning in a way other types of airplanes cannot. The question that focuses my nervousness is whether I have the capability. Lib and I agreed over the winter that we absolutely had to decide whether we were willing to spend the time and resources to make flying the Silent fulfilling and safe for me. We decided that I would take this July to find out. On every flyable day over the month I would drive down to London and fly the glider. Lib would come too, for general support, observation, and photo documentation, at least in the beginning. Even if my flights were brief, I would be practicing working through checklists, repeating the sequences necessary to get into the air, get around in the air, and get back on the ground. With familiarity would come competence and comfort, and we would have a clear idea of the time commitment.

I want to be practical. But I'm convinced this sailplane can give me something I really want, something presently just out of reach.

It's now July 22nd. For the last three weeks—eight trips to London—I have worked with the Silent on the ground. I have worked systematically—taxiing from one end of the long runway to the other, over and over, faster and faster. Now I can confidently lift a down-wing just off the asphalt with the ailerons and keep both wings level as I roll on the single main wheel. With the elevator I can raise the rear of the glider and level it as well, and steer straight down the runway with the rudder.

Between sessions with the Silent I have thought a lot about riding a bicycle. In both bicycle riding and ground-handling an airplane, complex hand-and-foot activity has to become second nature. It has to be something you can do under normal circumstances without thinking. That leaves your active mind free to deal with glitches—a stick in the road for a bicycle maybe, an unexpected gust for an airplane. It takes a lot of practice on a bicycle to get to that second-nature stage, though most people do it as children, so young they don't remember how it felt.

It has taken 71-year-old me a lot of taxiing practice to get to that stage with the Silent. Libby has watched patiently on the ramp through it all, offering encouragement when I taxi back in from practicing. Other pilots who use the airport have gotten used to dealing with the long-winged white sailplane taking up the whole runway as it cruises back and forth. I thank Lib and other pilots often.

On this Sunday morning—with no other pilots using the airport—I will add to my systematic taxiing a real take-off. There's no way to take off without subsequently landing, so I plan to climb to 2000 feet over the airport, shut the engine down and retract it, fly a few circles, set up a landing pattern, and land. If all goes well I will repeat the exercise. It will be kind of like a first flying solo experience, where you have to take off and land three times. There shouldn't be any of the epic "firstness" of that universally-momentous occasion, but this will definitely be a step toward figuring out whether I have a future with the Silent.

So I'm nervous when I pull our van up to the touchpad-controlled ramp gate at the London airport and enter the combination. The gate slithers aside and Lib and I drive out onto the asphalt, turning to enter the labyrinth of passageways separating the three rows of single-airplane hangars. The hangar I rent is number seven. I pull up, step out of the van, and let myself in.

I turn on the fluorescents and push the UP lever above the light switch to raise the massive folding door. Lib slips in under the rising door, cradling her camera. The morning light streams in over the glossy white sailplane and trailer. The hangar is large enough for the Silent to sit assembled in front, while the trailer angles 45 degrees out of the back recesses. Lib snaps a picture of me standing next to the glider in a shaft of light.

I place my dark glasses, hat, parachute, headset, and water bottle on a folding chair along the hangar wall and move to the glider. Lib sits on the adjacent chair. "Checklist," she says.

It's all too easy to pass through a repeated sequence of actions in a pro forma way. I've walked into this hangar and readied the glider a dozen times, but following a checklist—as both Lib and I know—makes actions mindful. It keeps me honest. I retrieve my preflight checklist from the cockpit. Ironically, checklist or not, I will always remember the ensuing chain of small actions of this day.

Kneeling by the side of the waist-high cockpit, I toggle to ON the master electrical switch, then the engine erection switch. An internal motor starts up with a high whine and almost invisibly-hinged clamshell doors behind the cockpit crack open. A pylon rotates out, a pylon supporting a single-cylinder engine that drives a thick, black-rubber belt. The belt loops through a reduction gear and turns a single-bladed propeller. I know that the propeller is precisely counter-balanced, that the purpose of the single-bladed design is to decrease the height of the pylon, that no thrust is lost with the single blade. But the single blade always looks broken to me.

Lib sits patiently. She knows not to interrupt me. Airframe, engine, instruments, fuel: I touch, wiggle, or peer thoughtfully at everything I can, checking according to the checklist. When I have completed it I pick up the parachute and the headset and stow them in the sailplane's seat. I am always impressed by the parachute's weight, though I probably wouldn't be if I ever had to use it. I slide a reflective canopy cover over the nose to keep the sun from focusing through the plexiglass like a magnifying lens, and I level the wings with a rolling wing stand. With hat and dark glasses on, I hook the rear tow bar into a removable tail dolly and steer the Silent out of the hangar into the sun.

"Watch the wingtip," Lib warns. I am watching the wingtip as it clears the hangar opening, but my eyes can't be everywhere and when Lib asks, "Is that gravel on the taxiway going to cause a problem?" I am grateful, stopping to sweep the gravel aside with my foot before pushing past. Out on the ramp I remove the wing stand, towbar, and tail dolly. Lib makes a neat pile of them on the grass beside the asphalt while I belt myself into the parachute and remove the canopy cover. I plug in the headset before levering myself into the cockpit, clicking in the straps of the four-point seatbelt harness, and pulling checklists from the compartment beside the seat.

Altimeter, belts, ballast, canopy, controls, wind direction, dive brakes, emergency.

I check, push-and-pull, and rehearse the elements sequentially, then do the same for the engine-start sequence.

From inside the cockpit, I take a deep breath.

"You'll do fine," Lib says, through the sliding vent panel in the canopy. "You're ready for this." She steps away as I toggle the master switch on, listening for the whine, watching the red ready-light come on. I pull the stick back to keep the tail down, pull the dive handle back to compress the wheel brake, pull the propeller stop lever back to allow free rotation of the prop. A mini-checklist of three "backs."

I press the starter button.

The engine behind my head explodes reassuringly into life. On the instrument console black numbers on the rpm meter rise to 2400. Outside Lib is turning in a standing circle, checking for anything else moving on the ramp, taxiway, or runway. I return her thumbs-up and take my hand off the stick to push the throttle forward. The engine note rises, the rpms advance to 3000, and the glider rolls forward.

I am confident now, in the moment and not nervous for the first time this day, back in the groove of taxiing. I rudder the glider across the ramp and out onto the east taxiway, along the center of the taxiway to the threshold of the runway. I stop then, pulling the throttle back and squeezing the brake. The push-to-talk for the radio is a red button atop the control stick. I push it and make an announcement to anyone who might be listening on the airport frequency.

London traffic. Motorglider six-zero-two sierra lima departing runway two-four. I will climb to two thousand and stay in the pattern for a full-stop landing. London.

Then it is onto the runway, square up on the center line, stop again while I look around and up one last time. Hand off the stick, I rotate the throttle all the way forward.

The glider surges and rolls, picking up speed fast. I have not experienced full throttle in all my recent taxi practicing, and I am gratified by how the glider comes alive and stable, rising off the asphalt almost before I have time for any conscious control inputs. I pull the stick back for a speed of 65 mph and rise steadily over the runway.

By the end of the 5700-foot runway, I am 500 feet up, banking left into a 180-degree turn. The glider is perfectly stable. The engine clatters away behind my head, the sound reduced by my headset, but still too loud for me to use the radio, either to transmit or listen. There is probably nothing to hear, though, no other pilot calling in who wants the use of the runway. I have it all to myself. I am feeling good.

Down the runway and back, the altimeter is up to 2000 feet. Time to shut the engine down. That is as simple as can be: just push the switch to turn off the fuel pump. The engine coughs and stops. Silence fills the cockpit. I hear a pilot calling on the radio from another airport. No need to keep up with him. I push the stick forward, lowering the nose of the glider to maintain 65 mph, and just sit for a moment, enjoying the view of the whole grass-and-asphalt airport stretched out below me, enjoying the silence, the stability and competence of the glider.

This is it. This is what buzzards feel on a calm, sunny day. This is what I want. Really want.

The engine is ticking as it cools off. I extend the propeller stop lever and blip the starter button. In a mirror on top of the engine console I can see the prop blade move about 70 degrees. Another blip and the blade contacts the prop stop and stops, vertical. I toggle the retract switch, the pylon motor whines, and the pylon rocks back in the mirror and disappears. Two seconds later I hear the thump of the closing clam shell doors. I am a pure glider now, flying nearly 40 feet forward for every foot I descend.

But I am noticeably descending. Retracting the engine always costs altitude. I fly two more broad circles over the airport just for the sheer joy of it, then set up for the downwind leg of a landing pattern.

I speak aloud the landing checklist mnemonic: FUSTALL. Flaps, undercarriage, speed, trim, air (dive) brakes…everything is where it should be.

I look carefully at the airfield below me. Nothing is moving, no airport calls on the radio during my short flight. I look down at the windsock in the grass off the ramp. Hardly any wind.

So now it's the final L: land. I just have to slide the glider back onto the ground.

I fly downwind down the runway, calm as can be inside and out. I go past the runway end about 45 degrees, looking back over my shoulder to keep the end in sight. I am a little bit high, so I open the dive brakes a little, bank 90 degrees left, the "base leg" of my pattern, a little more dive brakes, then another 90 degrees left and I am lined up perfectly with the runway. The dive brakes are about halfway open now, about right for an average landing, but I open them a little more so I can land short enough to turn straight onto the ramp.

I sink steadily toward the runway's end, aiming for the big 2 and 4 designating the runway's magnetic heading. Just as I pass over the numbers I pull back ever-so-slightly on the stick and the glider's glide levels out, the "flare" before touchdown. The touchdown itself is a little harder than I am expecting, but plenty smooth enough. I pull the dive brake handle back to fully extend the dive brakes and kill the wings' lift, then a little more to squeeze the wheel brake. The rear of the glider comes down as the speed drops, again a little harder than I am expecting. Some details to work out on my next flights.

The taxiway to the ramp approaches on my left and, releasing the brakes, I have just enough momentum to rudder left and off the runway. I push the push-to-talk button again.

London traffic. Motorglider two-sierra-lima clear of runway two-four. London.

I am suddenly aware that it is really hot in the cockpit. I have to get to the ramp.

Erecting the engine seems to take forever, though it is only about a minute. Master switch on, pylon up and locked, the three "backs," fuel pump on, starter button. The engine starts instantly. I push the throttle and roll down the taxiway onto the ramp.

Lib is standing to greet me. I push the fuel pump switch in to stop the engine, turn off the Master switch, rotate the latches, and raise the canopy. The gust of cool air that enters the cockpit is delicious.

Lib leans in beaming, handing me a water bottle and giving me a kiss. She understands that for the moment the only thing that matters to me is that I own a beautiful glider that I am certified to fly and finally feel pretty comfortable with, that in it I have soared like an eagle above the world.

As if to underscore the moment, the young airport employee who handles duties on the ramp roars up in his golf cart.

"Hey, Mr. Jones," he says. "I just saw your flight. I wanted to say how happy I am to see you in the air." I nod and smile. "I've watched you up and down the runway," he says. "You really put in a lot of work with that glider." It's a long speech for him. "It's really good to see you finally get into the air. It's a beautiful thing."

"You bet it is," I say.

He roars off. Lib is still beaming. "I'm really happy for you," she says. "You've sure earned it."

I think I'm smiling. I know I am really happy. Even the sailplane seems happy, wrapped around me with all its capable components, ready to go, like a thoroughbred racehorse. What seemed just out of reach before the flight—comfortably flying a sailplane that could take me up when and where I wanted, a sailplane that could satisfy my life-long yearning to soar independently—is right here, right now. I think Lib understands that for me right that moment all the yearning and earning has been worth it.

I think fleetingly of not flying again that day, of clambering out of the sailplane to give Lib a big hug and just savor the lovely moment. I would savor it all the way home, savor it that night, the next morning, and all moments until I fly again. But I know I should fly again right then, tighten up a few things about my landing technique, just enjoy the feeling of a complete flying experience one more time. Then we'll put the sailplane up and go home.

It will be oh so sweet.

Into the Air: Model Airplanes

As long as I can remember I have been excited by airplanes. I was born on an Air Force base, Wright-Patterson Field, in Springfield, Ohio, right at the end of World War II. My father was an Army Air Corps pilot. There is a family picture of me at about age three riding on a little sit-down metal scooter shaped like an aerial bomb, the body of it a tear drop with a square of connected fins at the back and four wheels at the bottom. I am sitting in the middle of the bomb, something like Slim Pickens on the A-bomb in that great scene at the end of "Dr. Strangelove." I am dressed in a light-colored sunsuit, a little strap-topped, short-pants number. My feet are on the ground, ready to push off and roll around. I'm smiling blondly and cherubically up at the camera. It's a strange image, when you think about it. I don't know what I or my parents thought about my pushing myself around on a bomb.

Before I knew anything about big airplanes, I knew about models. So did my father. He and his identical-twin brother were raised in Louisiana, in Baton Rouge, and were renowned model builders and flyers in the deep South during the 1930s. They won a lot of trophies at a lot of meets. There is an old newspaper story in the family album about "The Jones twins" and their recent success at a meet in Mississippi. The story has a picture of them holding a big "gas" model, its wide, long wings with their translucent covering shading their heads, its little engine and long thin propeller sticking gracelessly out its nose. They don't look identical to me, never have. But they do look very similar, and very confident.

There's another picture of me in the family album, perhaps from the same time as the bomb-scooter, as I am wearing what looks like the same outfit. I am sitting on the grass next to one of these big gas models, its wings dwarfing me, its clunky fuselage angling to the ground from two front wheels. I don't remember any of this, of course.

What I do remember is my grandparents' upstairs bedroom in Baton Rouge, where my brother and I slept when we visited there. This bedroom had been my father's and his brother's, and the walls and ceiling were hung over every available square inch with models. Small spaces held scale models of real airplanes, their solid surfaces opaque and brightly colored, emblazoned with insignias and letterings. Over beds and windows hung larger models with thin wings and long, floppy propellers. These were "rubber models," floppy propellers designed to fold back for gliding, extending under power from skeins of looped rubber. The lords of the room were two big gas models in the corner over the dresser. Like those in the photograph, their wings were a foot and a half wide in the center, tapering sharply out three feet in each direction to narrow elliptical tips, their engines wrapped in oily brown rags from which protruded malevolent-looking wooden propellers.

All the models were made of balsa wood, the wonderfully light, soft wood I now know is native to South America. Some of the solid scale models were carved and sanded from balsa blocks. All the larger models were "built up," with frames of balsa sticks covered either with thin balsa sheets, tissue paper, or silk, the fabric stretched drum-tight and painted with colored or transparent "dope," a plasticised lacquer well-known to model-builders. The room was a riot of significant shapes and colors, filled with the soft combined smell of wood, fabric, and dope.

This room full of model airplanes held endless fascination for me, as early as five years old. I wondered, for instance, why these particular models? Holding a scale model in my hand, I wondered what it meant about my father's taste that he had chosen to model this particular aircraft. What insight did it give me into his fantasy world as a teenager? How strange were images of my young father, long before he knew my mother, working at a building board, carefully, intently, his whole attention focused on a model I now held in my hand. How wonderful that I could look closely at the models and see how the balsa wood was carved, the delicate tracings of knife and sandpaper, brush strokes of colored dope, small unevenness in hand-painted numerals, everywhere the hand of my father.

Or was it the hand of his brother? I rarely knew who had built what. Nobody made anything at all of the distinction. I certainly could not see any systematic differences in craftsmanship. The gas models were my uncle's. This was common family knowledge and it fitted with their characters. My uncle was the louder, faster, more extroverted brother. The small scale model of the U.S.'s first operational jet was my father's. That was downstairs in my grandparents' house. What was the significance of its being downstairs? I never knew the answers to these questions, never even thought to ask them.

This busy and deeply evocative room still comes back to me in dreams, along with its characteristic smell. Wings come back to me in dreams too, big wings of gas models. Two other sets of these wings occupied the attic off this upstairs bedroom. One entered the "A" of this gable attic through a little door not five feet high. There were great arch-topped, iron-bound, dark wooden trunks here, filled, I knew from brief peeks, with old clothes and papers from my grandparents' youths, and some war mementos from my grandfather's WWI horse-artillery experiences. I remember sensing that these trunks were off-limits. I know they fairly pulsed with significance for me when I was five or six. Overhead, slid into the rafters, were the two great wings, seeming all the greater in the small space. They were the same sort as on the gas models hanging from the ceiling in the bedroom outside; but, separated from any fuselages, they seemed both more colossal and more poignant, large and significant structures inexplicably out of context.

I have other dreams of being in a barn-like structure, with pieces of full-sized airplanes standing, leaning, and hanging from massive framing timbers. The airplane structures are wooden too, but delicate. Some are covered in taut, tawny cloth. Others are not covered at all. There is no complete airplane anywhere. I am filled with an excited vision of putting a lovely airplane together and going flying. Even in the dream, though, I know this will never happen. I could never find all the pieces of a single, whole airplane. And all the structures are dusty and slightly damaged, fabrics punctured or slashed, frames cracked or broken.

My father left active duty in the Air Force, as it came to be called, after the war. He and my mother, my younger brother, and I returned to Louisiana until Korea erupted in 1952. My father got called back then, and our family ended up in, of all places, Puerto Rico. For most of the time we were there we lived in San Juan, in a little pink stucco house with Venetian blinds but no screens on the windows, built close to the street, across a sidewalk and a white, wrought-iron fence. We slept every night under tents of mosquito netting. My brother and I attended the Antilles Dependents School, with other military and diplomatic children.

My father had to fly a certain number of hours per month to retain his pilot's rating. So when he could take the time off from his duties training Puerto Rican WAFs (Women in the Air Force), he would go out on sorties with fellow pilots in AT6 Texans and fly around the Caribbean. I never saw him in one of these planes, but I always knew it when he had been flying. He would be charged up, eager to talk with my mother about the day's events, and laden with mahogany implements, like bowls and tongs. The flying was all over water, and this made him nervous. It made him more nervous that some of his companion pilots insisted on flying "right down on the deck," looking for big fish in the clear blue water and buzzing boats. Of course, the society of men being what it is, he would have to join them. "Your engine misses twice and you're in the water," he said on more than one occasion. The pilots would go to places like St. Thomas or St. Croix, shop and have a meal, and come back. They would buy hand-carved mahogany pieces made by local craftsmen—salad bowls, serving sets, horses' heads (prized as lamp bases), nut crackers shaped like women's lower torsos (hinged at the crotch), small tables, and chairs. The pilots returned with these things stuffed in the rear seats of the T6s.

My father got out of the Air Force in 1953. He said that if he stayed in, he was going to have to learn to fly jets, and he didn't want to do that. But in fact he had not really enjoyed flying for years, not since the war, I think. In the war he flew C-47s, DC-3s in their civilian connotation as the first commercial airliners that saw really wide use. He loved the airplane, loved its lines, loved its stalwart and dependable performance, but he didn't like many of the conditions under which he was forced to fly. The flying instruments and navigational aids available to pilots during the war were fairly primitive, the airplanes were slow, and when you had to fly, you had to fly. Much later, when my mother arose on a gray, rainy, windy day, she would say, "When your father woke up on a day like this, he would say, 'I'm glad I don't have to fly in this weather.'"

More than once I heard my father respond to questions about what he did in the war with, "I flew toilet paper coast to coast." But my mother always said, "He flew the generals." I know he flew transport, both people and materials. And I know he never went overseas. But we never had intimate "What did you do in the war, Daddy?" conversations in our household. There was, I guess, some unspoken constraint involved. It had been a very intense time for my father, and he never liked to talk about his emotions—never.

Part of the constraint had to be tied up with his twin brother's experiences. His twin was an Army Air Corps pilot too. He flew single-engined fighters, P-51s mostly, and was knocked down by flak in France flying bomber support on D-Day during the invasion of Normandy. He walked several days, almost all the way out of France, but he was captured near the Swiss border when he tried to ask for food. He spent the duration of the war in a POW camp and had a very bad time of it, with cold, hunger, and illness. My grandfather, grandmother, and father had a very bad time of it too during this period. There were just the four of them and they were very close. When I was growing up, nobody talked about flying in the war. The only story of my father's I have any recollection of involved flying over the Rockies, visibility negligible, ice on the wings, a rough engine, important people in back.

So I know my father did fly a lot of top brass around the country. I have his military overcoat, a great khaki thing overlayered with flaps, buttons, and belts. "That's what your father took with him when he was flying the generals," my mother said, whenever I wore it. I have always had the impression that my father got called on to fly these important folks because he was very dependable: safe, smooth, conscientious. It was always the lack of those characteristics that he complained about in other pilots he had to fly with after the war. But all this safe, conscientious, responsible flying took its toll. When he got out of the Air Force my father never wanted to fly again, and hardly ever did. Neither did his twin.

They didn't build model airplanes either, at least not for more than a decade after the war. I wanted very much, though, to build the kind of lovely, featherweight, balsa and tissue paper models that hung all over my grandparents' upstairs room. I built the first one when I was ten. It was a simple scale model of a Stinson Voyager, a high-winged, single-engined, tail-dragger sport plane. I built it from a kit--a one-by-three-by-twelve-inch box containing sticks and sheets of balsa wood, sheets of tissue paper, hardwood wheels and propeller, a few pieces of wire, and construction plans. All the surfaces of the model had to be individually constructed from sticks and shaped pieces cut from the balsa with a very sharp knife, pinned and glued together over the plans. The individual surfaces were assembled with more glue to make the complete airframe, which was knife-trimmed and carefully sanded. Tissue paper was cut to rough shape and stuck to the airframe with dope, trimmed with a razor blade, sprayed with water to draw it up tight, then brushed with more thinned dope to make it airproof. The construction technique was actually pretty similar to that for the real airplane, though its materials would be hardwood, metal, and fabric. My model had a wingspan of about a foot, and I brush-painted it Aeronca orange all over, against which the black numbers I stenciled stood out vividly. I knew it was rough and rickety compared to the elegance of the models in my grandparents' upstairs bedroom. But it was solidly enough made. It had the right feel and smell. It was flyable. It was definitely in the right tradition.

Shortly after I finished this model the Baton Rouge television station—the only television station—decided to have its first-ever promotional youth model airplane contest. This was not to be the kind of flying contest my father and his brother had been so successful in, but rather a scale model contest, judged solely on appearance. With some prompting from my father, I decided to enter my Stinson Voyager. Both of us felt it would fare well, as hardly any other children anyone knew about had entered into the labor-and-sharp-tool-intensive business of building stick-and-paper scale models.

I remember getting dressed up and being driven, somewhat nervous, my little orange airplane incongruous in my hands, to the TV station for the on-screen, live judging. I also remember being taken completely aback by the other entries lined up on the judging tables when I arrived. They were all "plastic models"—tiny models with precision-molded plastic parts—a whole wing or fuselage assembled like a clamshell. They were heavy, plastered with paint and decals, completely unflyable, yet some of them exquisite. Judged just on scale looks, my relatively large, ungainly, stick-and-paper model stuck out like a ragged pterodactyl in a crowd of sleek sparrow hawks.

I think my father was even more taken aback than I was. He didn't think of plastic models as "scale models" at all. They were toys. There was some serious error of category in this "model airplane contest," and he had led me into it. I understood this, and was not overly concerned when my model didn't score very high in the judging. And it didn't look too bad, I was told, on the black and white TV screen. But my Stinson Voyager was demeaned in my eyes. It was not a great scale model, and though flyable, it was not set up to fly. I wanted to build model airplanes that flew.

I have tried to think about why my father was so repulsed by plastic models, on this occasion and always. I can think of several reasons. One was a sense that the model was not really one's own work. The small, scale models my father had built were hand-carved from wood, sanded and smoothed, painted overall from scratch, and detailed—numbers, letters, insignia—by hand. A plastic model's parts were pre-molded. All you had to do was glue them together. Colored plastic eliminated overall painting. All the finish work was details, with decals for the numbers and insignia. Cheap thrills, my father would have thought. None of the creation of significant form from simple, basic materials by application of your human skill. Hand-carving models was a kind of engineering; my father was an engineer.

With built-up models like my Stinson Voyager the issue was even clearer. Here the builder was sharing in the essence of the real thing. Part of this was the construction process itself, the framing and covering roughly similar to that of the full-scale plane. But the essence of the real thing was that it flew, and the significant forms that took shape under the builder's hands in the kinds of models my father really respected shared this marvelous functionality. They shared the potential for the intimate relationship with the air that constituted flight, that made them parts of airplanes. I absorbed this, somehow. Scale appearance without function was a travesty. Flying was what it was all about. I turned away from scale models towards models that would really fly. And my father was happy to get back into model building as well.

For five years after that, building and flying model airplanes was our major family hobby. My father, my brother, and I were involved on an almost daily basis with building and testing models, and, in the summers, going to contests in several states around Louisiana. All the models we built were for "free flight," models we launched into the air by some means or other and then admired as they gave themselves up to the air in—we hoped—long, circling glides back to earth. Some smaller models we simply threw, pitching them with great baseball heaves straight into the sky, where they flipped gracefully over into glides. These became my brother's and my specialty, he with a better arm than I.

Rubber models like the ones in my grandparents' upstairs bedroom, with their floppy propellers and skeins of rubber, became my father's specialty. His foot-long folding propellers were works of art, their blades beautifully carved, sanded, and doped, their folding hardware carefully machined in the engineering shop at LSU. Contest airplanes carried typically 16 strands of quarter-inch-wide, one-sixteenth-inch-thick Pirelli rubber, imported from Italy. These muscular snakes of rubber were lubricated with the slipperiest imaginable mixture of castor oil, glycerin, and green soap, a mystery concoction whose formula my father kept secret. We kept the prepared rubber "motors" wrapped in wax paper, in a special ice chest at contests on the hot summer days: heat was detrimental to the rubber. Looped around hardwood pins running across the very back of the airplane's fuselage, these motors were wound with a hand drill. We stretched the rubber out the nose of the airplane two and three times its length in order to pack in 200 to 300 "winds." As we threaded the wound rubber back into the airplane, it erupted into great gobbets of knots, filling the fuselage when in place. A fully-wound, contest-quality rubber motor generated nearly a quarter horsepower at launch, and unwound for up to a minute, the great propeller making a steady loud hiss as the airplane climbed straight up into the sky. In the minute the rubber motor unwound, the airplane would be nearly out of sight. Even in still conditions such a model would take five minutes to glide down.

Some others of our models we towed aloft on strings like kites, running along with them on the fully extended strings until a gust of rising air plucked them off. Some were thrust aloft by tiny, solid-fueled rocket motors, with a sound like a bottle rocket on the Fourth of July and a trail of white smoke.

And then there were the gas models, for me the terrors of the skies. The free-flight gas models of my father's day were big, slow, often clumsy things. Those of my youth were sleek, screaming missiles. Engine and fuel technology had developed to the point where carbon-steel cylinders scarcely a quarter inch in diameter turned six-inch fiberglass propellers in a banshee screech 22,000 times a minute, pulling models straight up at more than 60 miles per hour. Clockwork timers limited the engine runs to ten seconds. Longer, and models would have climbed out of sight. From climb altitudes, pylon-mounted wings supported planes in seemingly endless glides. Classes of gas models ran to engines with full-inch-diameter cylinders and eight-to-ten foot wings. The guttural roar of their engines and their sheer size and velocity were overwhelming to my early adolescent self. I don't know that my brother ever built and flew a gas model. I stuck with the smallest two classes. But even so, you had to start that wicked little engine yourself, flipping its knife-sharp propeller with your bare fingers, adjusting the fuel flow for maximum rpms by turning a valve a half-inch from the screaming propeller, and holding the quivering plane up like a javelin to launch, with the hot, acrid engine exhaust whipping into your face. And with all this you had to remember, absolutely had to remember, at the very last second, to flip on the engine timer.

Getting model airplanes to fly properly was my first lesson in aerodynamics. The flight pattern we wanted was a nearly vertical, right-twisting climb, followed by a smooth transition to a flat, left-circling glide. Never did models fly this way "right off the bench." In gliding they would stall, or dive, turn too sharply or fly straight ahead. In climb they might veer off to the right or left, or worst of all, loop back into the earth under power, exploding into shards of balsa wood and tissue when they hit.

All models had to be "adjusted." We cocked engines, turned rudders, moved centers of gravity noseward or tailward, shimmed wings and tail surfaces. We practiced throwing angles for the hand-launched gliders, and warped their balsa sheet surfaces with steam. Every airplane was different, and obtaining the ideal pattern required different adjustments in each case, sometimes after every flight, as the surfaces flexed with temperature and humidity. But the principles that dictated the adjustments—the aerodynamic principles—were the same.

My father explained the principles to me early on, and instantiated them a thousand times in a thousand test flights and a thousand ensuing minute adjustments. The simple principles of fluid air flowing over curved surfaces, the variations in flowing velocity and the lifting and dragging of surfaces, all this became almost visceral to me. Watching an airplane I had built fly through a cycle of power and glide, I sensed, moment by moment, the complex mixture of forces as all its different surfaces moved through the air. In this early education in practical aerodynamics, I remember hearing the words "bernoulli," "venturi," and "pitot," but I was hazy about what they referred to. Were they nouns or adjectives? Effects or apparatuses? Apparatuses that worked because of effects? It never occurred to me that they might be names of people.

A hundred afternoons I watched our model airplanes with wonder as they wheeled high above our heads, taking long minutes to glide in their big counter-clockwise circles down from their engine, rubber, towline, or arm-powered launches, even in the dead air of late afternoons when we tested them. Their stately, circular, gravity-defying ballet never ceased to thrill me. They turned so surely and smoothly, seeming when they were high to be losing hardly any altitude, held securely aloft and sure in their turns by forces generated simply by their passage through the air, forces I took for granted. In contests, when we flew them for maximum times, they cavorted in the active mid-day air like swallows, bouncing and dipping on unseen currents, swooping hundreds of feet up, then spiraling sharply down, to level out and swoop up again. Sometimes they would simply circle up and up and up, out of sight into clouds. "It's in a thermal," my father would say, squinting up through his Ray-Bans. "Thermal" became a magic word for me.

Through all this empathetic model observation, I projected madly. What would it feel like to be in the model looking down, rather than on the ground looking up? What would it really feel like with the air under your wings, buoying you up? How would your tail feel, kicking around into a sweeping left turn, your wings banking, the horizon rolling around underneath you? I yearned for these sensations, yearned to fly myself.

I did get to fly a few times in these model airplane years between my tenth and sixteenth summers. My flying came courtesy of one of my father's best friends, John Capdevielle, "Uncle John" to me, in the southern tradition. Uncle John was in the pure Army in the war, and he flew little single-engined Piper L-series planes. He was the only one of my father's friends who joked about his own war experiences, and the only one who wanted to fly after the war, when I was growing up. During the times we were flying model airplanes, he was part of a partnership that owned a four-place Cessna 170, kept at the "downtown" recreational airport. He could hardly ever get my father to fly with him, though he asked him often. When none of his partners was available or interested, Uncle John would ask me if I wanted to "go up." I was the oldest male child among all his friends.

I certainly did go up with him whenever he asked. Just to be allowed in the dim, cavernous hangar, among the half-dozen or so very differently configured planes, was worth the trip. High wings and low wings, V-tails and double-tails, they were so quiet yet so purposeful, perched unnaturally on their wheels. All their broad, sweeping surfaces were designed not to roll but to fly. They were ready to go.

Walking out from the dim hanger onto the glaring, heat-soaked concrete apron was exciting too, traversing the row of tied-down planes, seeming much smaller outdoors than in the hangar. I liked the anticipation of the pre-flight check, moving the control surfaces, checking the fuel, the tires, the instruments. The Cessna was taut and jaunty with its nose in the air, and it was seductive to run my hands over its aluminum contours, thinking of the air soon to flow and the forces that would hold us aloft, smoothly swooping about in the sky.

I remember, however, being a little disappointed that there was so little swooping, that so much of each flight was like riding in a car. The engine was noisy, the cockpit cramped and busy. Much of the control of the airplane was via a steering wheel—a half-wheel, actually. One turned it around left and right, pushed it in and pulled it out. Rudder pedals replaced a car's accelerator and brake pedals: push in the left foot to turn left, the right foot to turn right. The plane bumped and bounced over the grassy field, and bumped and bounced almost as much in the super-heated, turbulent Louisiana summer air. Once we got to a reasonable altitude Uncle John would throttle back, loosen his seat belt, and let me fly the plane from the right seat. "Let's go off this way for a while," he would say, and I would turn in the appropriate direction and fly along levelly, learning to absorb the tribulations of the air with only minute movements of the wheel. We would fly out over the Mississippi River, over the stacks, flares, and gases of the petrochemical plants alongside it, out over the swamps and the bayous. Uncle John would point out landmarks, tell some stories of some of his flights in the war, and I would get to make a left turn here, a right there, finally a 180-degree turn to go home.

I do remember one exciting flight in which we flew over to the Atchafalaya Basin, a huge low, swampy area between the Atchafalaya and Mississippi Rivers. This was land designed and managed by the Army Corps of Engineers as a catch basin for flooding, should water rise so high as to endanger the levees that kept the Mississippi out of the countryside. I flew us to the Basin, but once there, Uncle John took over and dropped the Cessna down low over the miles of cypress and scrubby oaks. We could see egrets and white herons in tree tops, cattle grazing in higher areas, rivulets and sheets of water glinting everywhere, and an occasional fisherman, a local who wouldn't be lost in the webbed miles of indistinguishable waterways, probably running a trot line.

After my junior year in high school, my brother and I went off in other summer directions, and although my father and his brother occasionally still built a model, the glory days of summer contests were past. Uncle John's Cessna partnership broke up, and there was no flying or talk of flying in my father's circle.

Into the Air: Sailplanes

When I discovered the type of plane that would become my obsession for five decades, it was a surprise. I didn't go looking for it.

In the summer after I graduated from college, I got married, and my new wife, Libby, and I went over to Europe on a college charter flight for a ten-week honeymoon criss-crossing some dozen countries. Driving past a grassy, fenced field in West Germany one sunny afternoon, we saw a little knot of people right in the middle. This looked to me like a model flying group, so we stopped to see what was going on. What was going on involved not models, but a full-scale aircraft. It rested right on the bottom of its fuselage in the grass, one wing tip on the ground, the other up in the air. And what wings…longer and more slender than any I had ever seen on an airplane. As we watched from the fence line, the people standing around the plane moved back, the tilted wings leveled, what sounded like a car engine started up in a trailer across the field, and the airplane leapt forward, climbing steeply, towed by a cable coming from the engined-trailer.

It was just like the tow-line gliders my father, brother, and I flew as models, but this was full-scale. People were in this model! High overhead and off the line, the airplane—interior framework of its impossibly long wings clearly visible against the bright sky—floated into just the kind of broad, lazy circling our models were adjusted to do. And it was climbing, climbing in those lazy circles, clearly in a thermal. It climbed up nearly to the base of a cloud, then descended in more circles and s-turns, finally crossing the road right over our heads with a hearty whishhing sound to land in the grass on a single little wheel, half-buried in the bottom of its fuselage.

I was transfixed.

Libby and I found a gate to the fence and trotted out to the airplane. We were warmly welcomed, in spite of—or because of—my schoolboy German.

This was—we were told—a glider. And this was European-style glider flying: a wood-and-fabric airplane and a half-dozen people in a pasture on a sunny afternoon. In the trailer was a winch turning a drum wound with 500 yards of steel cable. The airplane sat two people, one immediately behind the other. Flights lasted about 20 minutes, time for a dramatic tow, a lazy climb, a relaxed descent, a whishhing landing in the soft grass, and another pair of flyers. I thought it was as close to flying model airplanes as it could get, with real people in the airplanes. It was a realization of my fantasies at age 15. I wanted it. But we had no money, no time that summer or on the horizon. We were going to graduate school in New York.

Gliding would have to wait.

Back in the U.S., in graduate school studying chemistry at the State University of New York at Stony Brook (now Stony Brook University), I built my first model airplane in seven years. It was a towline glider, one my father had flown very successfully in contests. I had always wanted to build it as a teenager but never gotten around to it. I got my father to send me the plans, bought balsa wood, and built it from scratch. Libby and I would take it over to a neighborhood schoolyard on still, late afternoons. She would hold it, launch it, and I would tow it up high, release it, and watch it circle slowly, majestically back down. My spirit, if not my body, glided down with it.

Another gliding window opened to me later that year when a friend brought me a copy of National Geographic, January 1967. "Sailors of the Sky," read the article title he showed me. And there, spread across the first two pages of the article, was a photograph to take my breath away: an all-white, smooth, slender, long-winged glider, flying towards the camera at a 45-degree left bank, the pilot tucked into the nose, smiling broadly out at the camera. Who wouldn't be smiling! Behind him towered the whole cloudscape of busy summer sky. "Alone with the wind," the caption said, "seven-time national soaring champion Richard H. Johnson of Dallas, Texas, rides the flowing mantle of a summer storm in his Skylark 4 sailplane."

Soaring! Sailplanes! Far more than just 20-minute lazy hops to cloudbase and back down, soaring, I read, was a full-service life in the air. People in sailplanes went hundreds of miles cross-country, filling hours with repeated climbs in thermals and inter-thermal descents. People soared close along the up-wind edges of the Appalachians. They soared high in down-wind air bounced over the towering Rockies. People soared along weather fronts, soared along cliffs at the edges of the sea, soared in hot air rising from cities. I was amazed.

I was also in graduate school.

The article mentioned the Soaring Society of America, the governing body for soaring in the U.S. Libby, sympathetic if not empathetic, procured a mailing address, and under the Christmas tree in 1968 appeared my membership packet and two issues of the Society magazine, *Soaring*. Fifty-eight years ago I became an Associate member of the SSA, the membership class for non-pilots. For 57 years, annually, I have renewed my membership, upgrading my status along the way. For 57 years *Soaring* has come every month. I read every word. Usually several times.

For 30 of those 57 years, Libby and I spectated at soaring. We visited commercial operations and club fields. We attended contests, including the first World Soaring Championships ever held in the US, in 1970.

It was a notable occasion.

The World Soaring Championships of 1970 were Libby's and my summer vacation that year. We drove down from New York to Louisiana, where my parents and most of my siblings still lived, and swapped our small, un-air-conditioned car for my parents' air-conditioned station wagon, complete with an inch-thick foam rubber pad filling the back. We drove all the way across Texas to Marfa, an old railroad town named after the daughter of a railroad baron, herself named after a character from Shakespeare. We drove, surrounded by the horizon, to an enormous, abandoned WWII bomber-training base, still looking abandoned when we were only 500 yards away. A world championships of anything? Libby was skeptical.

But there they were: the long tubular trailers, the long-winged gliders, gleaming white in state-of-the-art fiberglass, the murmur of voices from around the world. I cranked up my schoolboy German, and we wandered freely among the busy folks, pieces of gliders in various states of assembly strewn around us. We peered into tiny cockpits, glanced into the recesses of trailers, examined the official bulletin board with its international contestant list and imposing sectional map display. Out on the ramp I recognized names, both American and international, I had seen only in the pages of *Soaring* magazine. Libby and I spoke with the wife of the American champion as she weighed every ounce of ballast water in her husband's custom-modified, super-long-winged sailplane.

Clearly there was no one there but aficionados—pilots, families, officials, and retrieve crews.

We were there the next day when the contestants were all lined up in teams and introduced. We watched as some 60 gliders were rolled into position in rows of three on the endless weedy concrete, watched as the pilots—white-garbed to ward off the sun, sunglassed and bucket-hatted—lowered themselves far down into their cockpits and locked the huge plexiglas canopies over their heads, watched as half-a-dozen stubby, powerful, tow planes taxied into position, and, choreographed by a single man with a small orange flag, in quick succession pulled aloft the floating, wing-flexing gliders. In a half hour the sky was full of the wheeling crosses, glinting now white against the sun, now black in silhouette, all moving in great, intermixing circles.

An hour later the sky was empty. I felt empty too. I knew a lot about soaring, about the sailplanes and the men (almost all men) who flew them. But I was not a pilot. I didn't know how it felt to be part of the air. On this first day of the contest, as they would every day, the gliders departed on the day's task, passing at timed intervals across an imaginary gate in the sky and heading out to the first turnpoint. I, on the other hand, felt done for the day. I found myself singing in my head, over and over, Gordon Lightfoot's lines from his song, "Early Morning Rain": "This old airport's got me down/ It's no earthly good to me/'Cause I'm stuck here on the ground…."

The goal of the sailplanes out on the course was to fly east, then north, then west, then home again, turning at appointed landmarks, photographing each to prove they were there, going as fast as they could. Getting all the way around would require 375 ground miles. It would take over five hours for the fastest gliders. It would be a busy day in the cockpits.

Meanwhile, back at the Marfa airfield: nothing. Everybody got out of the sun, off the griddle of the concrete. Soaring is not a great spectator sport.

Libby and I headed for the hills, literally. During the days of the contest, after the group launch, we hiked around Davis Mountain State Park and Big Bend National Park. We watched the Rio Grande River apparently flow upstream. We watched a flash flood flow over the highway, understanding the purpose of the white stick markers with the red tops we saw everywhere at low points on the road shoulders. We tiptoed out of the car to look at saucer-sized tarantulas.

Back at the Marfa airfield at days' ends, we peered above the dancing western horizon. Suddenly the narrow, t-tailed profile of a glider would emerge, black within the shimmering air. Finishing low and fast, using all their precious altitude in high-speed, fiercely whistling runs through the imaginary finish gate, the gliders would pull up into great arcing turns, parallel streams of ballast water misting from their wings. Momentum expended, they would circle, drop, and flare to float along just above the runway, touching down finally like goose down on snow.

The nights of the contest we stayed in the campground at the park on Davis Mountain. We slept the first night on the ground in the open until we were nosed by what, to our myopic night eyes, looked like black and white cocker spaniels. Glasses on, we saw skunks larger than we ever imagined existed. We vaulted into the back of the station wagon, grateful for the thick foam pad. Later, when the sand started blowing and a thunderstorm came, we were even more glad to be under roof.

I learned from this world championship at Marfa, have learned from other contests and from reading *Soaring*, that the terrain and meteorology best for soaring are generally not good for other activities. I have learned that non-soaring companions on soaring outings live martyred existences, passing time in harsh environments listening to aircraft radios, waiting to see if their pilots make it back from the days' flying, or, done to earth by weather, bad judgment, or both, are in need of "retrieval." Then, towing the long trailer behind the Chevy Suburban, they drive far off the beaten path, find the pilot in a farmer's field, disassemble and load the glider into the trailer, then drive back through the night to the home airfield while the pilot sleeps in the back seat. I have learned the names and faces of America's top pilots, the names and configurations of sailplanes, the names of instrument makers, of parachute companies, of insurance underwriters. On countless airline flights, as the immense airborne buses hurtled up to cloudbase, I have transported myself imaginatively into the cramped cockpit of a white, long-winged bird, circling as part of the air, looking down on the world slowly wheeling past below.

But there was never time for a real sailplane.

Time was for graduate school and for college teaching. By 1976, I was a full-fledged historian and philosopher of science, having achieved a Ph.D. from the University of Chicago, focusing on Conceptual Foundations of Science, and a real job teaching the same at the University of Tennessee in Knoxville. It was the time for first and then second children, for soccer, Boy Scouts, music lessons, Libby's and my students, books, papers, conferences. From my graduate education, I had learned some things about flight: the early history of continuum mechanics and the Bernoullis who made it a science. And I continued reading *Soaring* magazine. I may have been the best-read soaring-wanabee pilot in the world!

I bided my time, my memories, my imagination.

In grad school, I did find some time for another kind of model glider, a radio-controlled model. I built in the traditional stick-and-paper way a scale model that was much too fragile, then a workhorse entry-level plane, covered with heat-shrink plastic film. That glider proved wonderfully satisfying to fly, catapulting skyward above college athletic fields with 20 yards of rubber surgical tubing and 300 feet of nylon line.

Off tow, the glider was a bird of my own. I could bank it into a soft turning pattern and let it float the field, searching for lifting air. I could arrow it off under a soaring buzzard, to turn in the thermal that omniscient airborne wizard had found. I could turn and climb with the buzzard, past the buzzard up toward the clouds, until my eyesight and confidence in the range of my radio failed, and I cranked the turn into a hard spiral to bring the glider home. I could dive and swoop and play in the air. My hands were on the sticks, my eyes peered up, but my soul was in the air, looking out and down, and the air was under my shoulders, surging and dropping. My racing heart and my body language gave me away, I'm sure.

But it wasn't the real thing.

The real thing would have to wait some 30 years for a week at the Bermuda High Soaring School.

First Flight

It is 1998. I am bumping along in the passenger seat of a rusty golf cart along with Gil, our 17-year-old son, who stands amid the golf-bag fasteners behind the seat. It's South Carolina mid-March-cold—42 degrees—and a stiff wind is blowing into our backs. The sky is clear, hard blue.

All around us are piney woods: 20-foot skinny pines and 10-foot scrubby oaks, their bark grey and gnarly. Manila sand and dusty orange-red soil heave in hummocks and troughs like a dune area, which is what this was, however many thousands of years ago.

We are rolling down a narrow field carved out of the woods, tussocky under a thin buzz-cut of grey grass. The golf cart lurches silently among the bumps. I hear the wind rasping around my ears and the soft, deep-toned, irregular metallic bumps and booms, in delayed synchrony with the bumps of the cart. That's the sailplane.

We are pulling the sailplane along behind us. It's tilted over on one wingtip, canting on a bent, springy wire. The fuselage rolls on a single tire about the size of the tires on the golf cart, which now lurches into a low spot and lurches out. A moment later I hear the oil-drum boom of sheet aluminum as the sailplane navigates the same depression. The field is 4000 feet long. It's taking a while.

The cart driver is Jim Gager, our instructor. He introduces himself as just "Gager." He's lean, six-foot plus, with a weathered, squinty face under a faded red baseball cap. Gager's outer layer is a zip-up insulated body suit, blue-worn-to-grey, with red-and-white striped bands on the upper arms. "Piedmont" is stenciled prominently above the right front pocket. I wonder if the suit reflects his former employment. I know, in that suit, he is warmer than I am.

Gager, we learned this morning in the Bermuda High Soaring School clubhouse, has been soaring for only three years. He came out to this very field with a gift certificate from a girlfriend for a glider ride. He stayed on. Right through his solo, his private and commercial certificates, his certificate as a flight instructor. Everything is very familiar to him. Everything is still interesting to him too, even a little wonderful. He seems happy to be here. I sense a mid-life crisis successfully resolved.

We pulled the glider out this morning from a hanger full of its kin, a three-dimensional grid of angled, white geometry, long wings going every which way and fuselages—their noses close-cloth-covered and blind—resting low on their little single wheels. This two-place training glider has high wings tied with struts to the lower fuselage, and a spartan, antiquey-looking cockpit. We pulled it gingerly, like a pick-up stick from a leaning pile, from the network of wings and tails, rolled it out the 30-yard long, accordion-doored hangar front, and went over it with a fine-toothed comb.

We probed vents and access holes, prodded pushrods and control cables, flexed movable surfaces. "The pilot-in-charge of the airplane takes his life in his hands," Gager told us. "It's your responsibility to make sure the plane is safe." "Ohh-kay," said Gil, on the rising inflection he has adopted since we last saw him at Christmas. It's his first spring break home from college. I am alert to changes in him.

We must be far enough down the field with the golf cart now, for Gager wheels it around all at once to pull up facing the glider. He reaches with his foot under the nose and kicks the tow hook open, dropping the towing loop to the ground, then rolls the cart and us 20 yards off to the side of the field, near a maroon and white truck. I can't think what this truck is doing here, but I have no time to ask. "All aboard," Gager says.

We stride back to the glider. It has been established in our instructional chat earlier that I will take the first flight, the first flight of the day, the first glider flight of my life. I think that I should not be nervous. Intellectually, I know everything that is going to happen. I have, after all, been a member of the Soaring Society of America since 1968, have read every issue of *Soaring* magazine since then. I have been waiting for this flight for 30 years, waiting with considerable commentary. Gil has heard me talk about soaring since he has heard anybody talk about anything. I'm supposed to know what I am doing, so I am as matter-of-fact as I can manage.

Aspects of the situation seem very odd to me though, almost surreal. The glider strikes me as a big model airplane. It's that slight, simple and unadorned. But though it is big for a model airplane, it doesn't seem big enough for two people to fly in. The cockpit is tiny, and far forward, right at the nose of the plane. There's a lot of airplane behind one here. It's hard to see it as a balanced arrangement. The glider's aluminum skin is starkly cold. And the day is so windy. I wouldn't fly a model in this wind. I feel very exposed, very much a creature of the ground, standing in the middle of this grass-bald field with this motorless model airplane, facing into a hard
blue sky and a stinging cold wind. It doesn't feel much like my fantasies of leaping into the warm, beckoning undulations of the air.

But Gager is giving orders, getting set to turn the glider into the wind.

"Roger, push down on that handle on the nose. Gil, push on the left strut. There's nothing under us but sand. If we just pivot the plane on its wheel, we'll screw it right into the ground. So keep it rolling." We all push; the glider rolls and turns. It is light, easy to handle.

"OK, Roger," says Gager, tilting the cockpit canopy all the way over to its left, hinged side. "Put your foot here, on this step, and swing in. Step down inside anywhere you want. Put your hand anywhere you want too, except on the canopy." I put my right foot on the step, lean in. The canopy is the only obvious place to put my hand, but I put it on the hinge edge instead, which is sharp and unpleasant. I swing my left leg over and step onto the seat, my right leg following onto the floor, and sit down, very upright, on the seat where I was just standing. Not a very graceful entry. Is there a better way? The sides of the glider are at my shoulders.

"This seat belt is more complicated than you're used to," says Gager, calmly. He seems to have all the time in the world. I, on the other hand, feel rushed, as though I am holding people up. Who? There's nobody out here but Gager, Gil, and me. But I'm fumbling with the belt, trying to see how it works.

Gager seems to levitate himself effortlessly into the back seat of the glider and speaks over my shoulder.

"You can put the canopy down if you want to," he says. I want to. The wind is blowing right in my face. I rock the canopy down to the right side, ducking instinctively. Surely it will be too low for my head. But it's not. I notice that the scene is not distorted in the plastic, as it was looking through it from the side. I notice that it is much quieter, and immediately warmer. I pivot and slide forward the odd-shaped bent-wire canopy latch, noticing that the bend makes a good place to stick your finger to operate the thing. So much to notice. I think that one day all these little things will be unnoticed, will recede completely into the background, as so much associated with getting into and out of my car is. But now it's all fresh. It's the first time. I want to be conscious of noticing everything. But Gager is going on.

"Now we've got this little checklist placard, up there on the left side of the panel. Let's use it to go over the instruments and controls." We have covered this information in our classroom instruction earlier this morning. But I'm glad to have the time to look around. The cockpit scene is more hard-edged, more dingily functional than in the illustration we looked at this morning and in my life-long fantasies borne of *Soaring* magazine articles.

"Altimeter." With a little knurled knob at the bottom of the businesslike black-and-white dial, I set the two hands of the altimeter straight up to zero, close enough to the field elevation in eastern South Carolina. The air speed indicator is to its right, across the top of the panel. Below it is the variometer, which depicts how fast the glider is going up or down.

"Belts." I have figured out the seatbelt and fastened myself in.

"Canopy." Down and latched. Yes it is.

"Controls and Trim." I push the left rudder pedal in; the right comes out. Right in, left out. I don't know what I'm supposed to notice about this. Certainly they move freely. I grab the stick with my left hand, remember that I have to use my right one, switch, and push the stick all the way forward, pull it all the way back. Don't know what I'm supposed to notice here either, except, again, free movement. I push the stick all the way left and look at the left aileron deflect up, swivel and see the right one down. Right stick, opposite effect. At least I can see these guys move.

The bare metal, ratcheted trim lever on the floor between my feet, is supposed to be all the way forward, Gager tells me. It is, and it's a good thing. It would be tough to reach it with these belts tightened up like this. I think that this may not be the best order for this checklist.

"Cable." I'm supposed to check that the cable is hooked up and the tow release is locked in. The tow release is a worn red knob, bigger than a golf ball, smack in the top-middle of the panel. I pull it out a couple of times, careful to use my left hand, against a strong spring.

"Dive brakes." That's a half-inch steel rod with a right-angle bend in the far end, on the left side, above my knee. It slides back and forth when the right-angled end is pivoted out. Pulling it back, I look left and see the panel in the lower surface of the wing tilt out. I notice it's red-painted on the side facing me. So I can see it, I guess.

"When the handle is all the way back," says Gager, "the wheel brake is engaged. You don't want to land like that." OK. I feel the springiness in the last couple of inches of travel. Otherwise, the handle stays where you leave it. I ask Gager if you have to hold the handle in position when you're flying, if the air flow tends to push the spoilers closed or suck them open. He doesn't want to stop to talk about that. What should I ask about? What not? I guess I'll just not ask about much of anything.

I am conscious that my questions are motivated partly by genuine curiosity, partly by a sense of asserting myself, of showing Gager I'm slightly knowledgeable, that I'm thinking about things. But Gager is moving on. He wants to show me how to pivot the right-angled rod down when it's fully forward, to lock the spoilers closed. I can't help myself. I think of all the commentary I have read in *Soaring* about the problems associated with taking off with spoilers open, about the controversy among flight instructors and tow pilots over a tow-plane signal for "spoilers open." Is it a rudder-waggle? What are the pros and cons? I can't remember exactly. No way I'm going to bring this up, purely showing off. But I've got to shut down myself thinking like this! We have come to the bottom of the list on the placard.

"OK," says Gager, swinging a little door open behind me, getting out of the glider. I look up and see the tow plane, a hundred yards away, rolling toward us down a slope in the field.

"Who's the tow plane pilot?" I ask, not really able to think who it might be. In the office this morning were only Gager and Jayne Reid, co-owner of the operation. Her husband, Frank, I know is gone for the day, talking to the FAA in Charlotte. I read about another tow pilot on the Bermuda High home page. Did he come in while we were getting the glider out here and going over it?

"Jayne," says Gager, matter-of-factly. "She's the chief tow pilot."

I am genuinely surprised, and then embarrassed that I am so surprised. I remember that Jayne was mentioned as a tow pilot on the home page too. But my image of her is talking to me on the phone, receptionist-friendly. I think of her signing all the letters to us. She was clearly managing the office this morning, answering the phone, doing paperwork. But here comes this narrow-cockpitted, low-slung, angular, bow-legged power plane, this ex-crop-duster, chuffing down the field toward us like some powerful, shortlegged bully; and Jayne is driving it. Whoa.

Shiny blue and white, the tow plane approaches on our left, sweeps around in a dramatic 180-degree turn 20 yards in front of us, and sits, slightly off to the right, motor and prop running. I catch a glimpse of Jayne in the narrow cockpit as it sweeps past: high collared coat, big turquoise headphones, wrap-around dark glasses. I think first that she looks like some central casting WWII pilot. But wait. Turquoise headphones?

I see the yellow towline in an arc on the ground in front of us. Gager walks over and grabs it, passing it around his back. He motions to Gil, who trots over to him. The tow plane engine roars up and it rolls forward, the towline slipping around Gager's back, the silver tow hook bouncing and twisting along the ground. With three yards of line left before the end, Gager stoops down and the tow plane stops. Gager carries the line over to the nose of the glider, under me, and he and Gil fumble around.

"Pull the knob," says Gil.

I pull.

"Let it go," says Gil, and I do.

They stand up, and the tow plane engine roars again, taking out the slack. Gil stoops down and the tow plane stops.

Gager levitates back into the glider and swings his door closed. Gil moves out to the left wingtip.

"OK," says Gager. "Let's do the checklist again."

I am tempted to sigh, but I read the placard again out loud: altimeter, belts, controls, trim. I stop on "cable." I presume Gager and Gil handled the cable appropriately. Is this a test? How am I supposed to know? I think that this checklist really leaves something to be desired. Let's see, should you do all the other stuff before you hook up the tow cable, and then establish a verbal confirmation from the hooker-up now, at this step? I really don't have time to think about this.

"The knob's in, anyway," I say, sort of weakly.

"Dive brakes." Last entry. A separate entry, I notice. I demonstrate that the spoiler lever is all the way forward, locked down. I look out the canopy at the wings, left and right, checking the spoiler panels. I haven't felt this way since my driver's license road test: adjust mirrors, check handbrake. Stop thinking about how you're feeling! Well, maybe not. Remember: these feelings, these first feelings, are precious. I'm only going to get to do this for the first time once.

"Give him a thumbs up," Gager says, meaning Gil. I do that. Gil bends down and lifts the wing about chest high. That's not enough to level the glider.

"That's not high enough," says Gager. But Gil can't hear him, and Gager can't figure out how to signal Gil, and the tow plane is roaring again. "Oh well, we can deal with it," says Gager evenly, as the glider starts to move.

I think about water skiing. The book we read this morning talked about the analogy between a boat's towing a skier and the tow plane's towing the glider, how the skier can't pull himself out of the water, but should just sit back and wait for speed to build up, and how the glider pilot likewise shouldn't try to pull back on the stick to get the glider up, but just let the glider take off on its own. I'm not holding the stick, of course, and I'm not thinking about the specifics of the analogy. But I did a lot of water skiing when I was young, and that is the only experience I have to put against this one. I remember well the tremendous forces you get on a slalom ski when the boat first starts to move, when you're way down in the water. What are the forces going to be here?

I am still waiting to get some feel for the analogy when things start to happen really fast. The glider bumps and slews along the ground. The stick between my legs jerks back and forth wildly, banging into my thighs. I try to move them up, out of the way, but there's nothing to put my feet on. A horizontal tornado of dried grass all at once flies back at us from the tow plane's prop wash and I duck instinctively as we pass through it. The grassy ground in front of us speeds up, turns into a blur that makes me dizzy.

"This bumpiness will quit as soon as we get off the ground," says Gager. But it really doesn't. The glider gives a kind of lurch upward, then continues to bounce and slew. The bounces and slews are slower, but even more extreme. The tow plane rises off the ground, and we rise behind and slightly above it.

I am overwhelmed. The roar of the tow plane and the sound of rushing air fill the cockpit. The glider lurches up and down, one or two seconds a lurch, my stomach lurching a beat behind. The tow plane rises and falls in front, out of synchrony with the lurches. We roll from side to side, less extensively than we lurch, but still out of sync with the tow plane. We slew back and forth, and now the tow plane is adding to the chaos by starting to turn right.

"We want to keep the nose aimed at the tow plane's outer wingtip," says Gager, from the back, in the most normal sort of tone. I had forgotten all about him, forgotten that someone was actually flying the glider. I think with astonishment that my sense was that we were just being dragged willy-nilly behind the tow plane. "...keep the tow plane wings lined up with the lower edge of the canopy," Gager is continuing.

"How you doing?" he asks.

"I'm OK," I say, trying a little rueful laugh that comes out more like a shudder. "It's just ... all so fast," and I want to add, so extreme: so much motion, so many forces. But I sense that Gager only wants to know if I am in imminent danger of throwing up, or something that would require action. He is not interested in my impressions.

I barely have any sense that we are "high," that we are in the air. I look down briefly but don't have any visceral reaction. It might be a video background. There's just this incessant lurching, rolling, and slewing, now more, now less, and the tow plane rising and falling, banking and intermittently turning, always slightly below us, the towline arcing yellow from its tail to my feet.

"We're passing through 2500 feet," announces Gager, and I look down at the panel, taking a moment to locate the altimeter—upper left—noticing as I scan that the variometer needle is halfway above horizontal, into its "up" range. Sure enough, the little white hand of the altimeter is on the white "2" and the big hand is sweeping slowly past "5."

"When we get to 3000, reach out and pull the tow release, the big red knob," says Gager. I'm a little crestfallen that he added that last instruction. "Give it a good yank. We'll do a right turn then, and the tow plane will do a left."

The little hand is not quite to "3" when Gager says, "OK, pull it." I do, making sure to use my left hand, as I will when I have to fly the glider with my right. There's a loud metallic bang, and four things happen at once, all of them disconcerting to me. The tow line turns from a smooth arc to a series of s-es, disappearing below us; the tow plane falls away to the left; my body lurches up and forward, my stomach following an instant later; and the glider falls over in a right bank.

Before I have time to worry, it rights itself, levels out, and everything is a lot smoother. The noise is considerably less, there's no lurching and slewing, and nothing is moving in my canopy-enclosed field of vision. It's just the blue sky above and green earth below. I am conscious that my heart and my breathing are fast. My muscles are tensed; I am trembling slightly. I take a deep breath.

"Notice the horizon," says Gager. "Take a little Kodak snapshot of it." By this I know he means, "Freeze the image in your mind's eye." He used the same phrase this morning in our instructional talk, and I thought he was actually going to take a Polaroid picture at this point, to give me to keep for a reference.

What I notice is that the horizon is about one-third of the way up the pitot tube just in front of me, outside the canopy. There's a tuft of yarn blowing from the pitot tube, the "yaw string." The horizon is a little below that. I freeze the description, if not the image.

"That's about 50 miles per hour," says Gager, "the air speed for the best glide ratio of this glider." We covered that this morning. I look for the air speed indicator: upper right. Below it, the variometer says we are going down. The altimeter says 2500. We've already lost 500 feet.

"Now I'm going to make a left turn," says Gager. The glider banks sharply to the left, then the stick comes back smartly into my upper right thigh. The glider levels out.

"Look down," says Gager. "Can you spot the field?" I see it right away, to the left and in front of us. I point, sort of lamely. Gager can't see me pointing, I know.

"We want to stay out here, upwind of the field," he says. "Now we're going to make a right turn."

The glider banks sharply right, the stick comes back smartly into my upper left thigh, and suddenly we are thrust upward for a long second. My stomach lurches downward; my whole body slumps downward.

"Boy, that's a strong thermal." Gager's voice indicates some genuine enthusiasm here, and I am grateful for this slightly out-of-the-ordinary circumstance. The gap between his all-in-a-day's-work nonchalance and my overwhelmed state is a little discouraging to me.

"I'm going to hold this right turn a little and slow down. Let's see if we can't gain a little altitude here." The right bank makes me feel slightly like I am falling. But the force upward tells me we are rising. It's a daunting mix of sensations. As I try to process the mix, we lurch more strongly upward, and Gager says, "Whoa. We just gained 600 feet." I mistakenly look at the variometer instead of the altimeter, noticing the hand above horizontal. The big hand of the altimeter in the opposite up corner of the panel points to "9," I see.

"So, my first thermal," I say. "My first flight and I'm already soaring." I try to sound a little thrilled, but my voice is shaky. I hope it doesn't sound sarcastic. I know that I am supposed to be thrilled. This is my lifelong dream! People who write to *Soaring* magazine all say they were thrilled on their first flight. But I am just too shaky. I don't exactly want it to be over, but I have a sense of just kind of holding on.

We level out and fly straight for a while. Though the sky is completely blue and there is no sign of any activity in it, every three or four seconds we balloon up or down. I think that I had no idea, all these years of looking up at the sky, that there was this much going on up here. The sailplane balloons up, and all of me goes down, stomach first, everything else following. The sailplane is crushed down, and all of me rises, stomach in the lead. All I can think about is my body and my stomach. But Gager is pointing out landmarks.

"The field is down to our right. You can see the clubhouse about halfway down it. At the end is a church. See it?" I look at the end of the field, a clutter of buildings. It takes me a second to make any sense of them.

"Oh yeah. I see the steeple," I say.

"That's going to be important to us," says Gager, a little portentously. "Across the road there is an open area we call the horse farm. There really are horses there, but that doesn't matter. It's just a way to identify it. And here on the right is what we call the gold mine." It's a big open-pit, manilla-red layered gash in the green ground. Hard to miss.

What Gager doesn't mention is what seems to me the most obvious aspect of the landscape: an enormous curtain of purple-brown smoke some miles away, arising in a line from the ground and going straight up, until the top is blown away diagonally.

"What about that smoke over there," I ask, when it is clear Gager is not going to bring it up.

"That's probably a controlled burn from the wildlife area," says Gager. My mind is flooded with questions irrelevant to our flying: What wildlife area? Why a controlled burn on such a windy day as this? State or federal area? I don't ask any of them.

"Probably a big thermal over there with that," says Gager. Everything is to be identified according to its role in the soaring scene, I think.

I ask, "Wouldn't you have to worry about toxic fumes or something in the glider if you went into something like that?" Again, I ask it less because I want to know—certainly I already know what sort of answer one would give—but to show I am engaged in the experience and not just thinking about my stomach.

"Maybe. But when you get desperate, you'll look for lift anywhere," intones Gager. Sounds like the voice of one who might have been desperate once or twice. In any case, the smoke is not a landmark, not relevant to our situation right here. We will ignore it.

We make some more turns. This is all lasting a lot longer than I thought it would. And every turn is an adventure—the initial bank, with my stomach sinking into it, the stick opposite, back against my thigh, the level out, the little release of tension.

"Now we're going to be aiming right at that church," Gager says, and I am suddenly aware that we are beginning a landing approach. I had been paying no attention at all to the altimeter and could not have said that we were particularly lower than we were however long ago.

The nose of the glider points down a little. There is a slight rushing sound in the cockpit. The frequency of lurches and slews increases.

"I'll pull the spoilers out a little," I say. The rushing sound increases, the glider decelerates, and I feel my body falling forward. We are headed straight to the church. I fix my gaze on it.

"We want to be at about 800 when we pass the clubhouse," says Gager. The clubhouse? Oh yes, it must be straight out on our right. I detach my eyes from the church, look over the right side. There is the clubhouse. I look at the altimeter, but we are already well past the clubhouse by this time. The big hand is below "8." Where is the little hand? We are almost over the church.

"We want to be at 500 when we get to the church," says Gager, in the same even voice, always the same even voice. Should I look at the altimeter again? The church is right below us.

"Now we're going to make kind of a steep right turn," he says, already beginning what clearly will be the most dramatic maneuver we have made the whole flight. We tilt crazily over. The nose is pointed way down at the ground. My body feels like it is just flat falling out to the right. The ground is coming up fast.

"We'll go down the road a little," says Gager, and I look down for the road. "And make another right turn." I have barely absorbed the road and the glider is already tilting crazily over again, nose pointed even more sharply down.

"I want to be sure I clear the trees," intones Gager, way above the trees flashing below us, while we sink like...like what? It feels like we're not flying at all, just falling like a big soggy leaf.

As we get nearer the ground, the feeling of falling is overwhelmed by the visual impression of fierce linear speed: the ground is running beneath us madly, the grass a gray-manilla textured blur.

"We look down the field as we get close to the ground," says Gager solemnly from behind me. I am tense all over. I have never gone this fast this close to the ground, I think. I try to look down the field, up over the rise to the clubhouse on the left. Suddenly the wheel touches, there is a cacophony of muted banging and bumping, and we decelerate more quickly than I would have thought possible. As we slow, the tail of the glider comes up behind us, the nose goes down. We stop smoothly. As the tail comes down with a thunk and the glider slowly tilts over to the left side to rest on the wingtip, I see the maroon and white truck. We are back where we started, very near the downwind end of the field. How could we have used so little field in stopping? It is quiet and still.

My body doesn't know what to do. The sudden quiet and still is almost as disconcerting as the overwhelming sensations that preceded it. I feel weak, limpid, transparent. I am struck by the hard constancy of the glider. It is solid, immovable, the metal sides and panel hard and bright, the instruments official black and white. It's unfazed, the same as when we left. But I am not. I am a jellyfish, inconsequential. The whole flight...so much; so fast. How is it possible to take it all in, much less control it? I think of the immense distance in coordinated experience between where I am now and where I need to be to fly the glider. Where Gager is, who has taken it all in no-sweat stride. All these thoughts take, maybe, three seconds.

"Was it fun?" Gager asks, in a friendly way.

"`Fun' is a word, that...that doesn't even begin to...to have any relevance to it," I stammer. I want to say that it's a category error to apply the word "fun," but recognize that philosophical jargon would be wildly inappropriate. "It's all just so fast, so many things happening, so many forces involved. I just...I just didn't think it would be quite that...much of everything."

"You want to go again?" Gager asks, being helpful, surely at least a little aware of how blown away I am.

"Sure," I say, a little bravely. "At least I'll know a little better what to expect this time."

Gager gets out of the glider behind me. Gil has come over. I notice that his blue nylon coat is zippered all the way up to the top. He stands to my right, looking into the cockpit.

"How was it?" he asks. Is he looking at me a little bemusedly? Do I look zonked?

"It's overwhelming," I say. "A whole lot happens really fast. There's a lot to do all the time. The air is much more turbulent than I had any idea of. This is going to be some kind of a thing." It comes out in a rush. "I'm going to try it again. You OK?" I have a little energy left for fatherly concern. I know it's got to be cold, just standing around.

"It's cold out here," says Gil, matter-of-factly. "But I'm OK with it."

The tow plane has come chuffing over, is making its sweeping turn, in front of us. Gil produces from his right coat pocket an odd-shaped wire implement flying a bright pink ribbon. He trots over to the yellow towline, picking it up in the implement, a kind of hook, I see. Where did he get this? He holds the line up in the hook and the tow plane roars off, the line passing through the hook in Gil's hand, the tow hook on the end of the line approaching rapidly from Gil's left, bouncing along the grassy ground, flinging up pieces of grass here and there. Abruptly Gil stoops, in an unnatural sort of way, and the tow plane instantly stops. I realize that this is a signal. Gil must have learned all about this while I was flying.

Gil brings the tow hook over to the nose of the glider and he and Gager fumble.

"Pull the knob out," says Gil. I pull it out, hold it out. This is already familiar, from the first flight.

"Let it in." I do. Both Gil and Gager stand up. Gager gets back in the sailplane while Gil looks out at the tow plane. The slack snakes out of the tow line. Gil abruptly stoops again, and the tow plane stops. He moves off to the left wing tip.

We go through the checklist again. No sighing this time, though I do notice that—already—I think about every detail less.

"Give Gil the thumbs up," says Gager, and I look over at Gil and do. He raises the wingtip all the way to wings level this time. Holding the wing with his right hand, he looks down the field at the tow plane and windmills his left arm. I look down field too at the little blue and white plane, hear the engine roar, see the dust and chaff kick back behind it, and feel the sailplane start to move. I move my legs up a little as the stick flails back and forth. The bumps are less dramatic. The slewing seems more controlled. My stomach is still lurching up and down, but the asynchrony with what I'm seeing is not so bad. The grass becomes a blur again, but I look up before I get dizzy. We lift off in no time.

Already, just the second run, this is going to be a lot easier, I think.

Halloween: Open Canopies and Falling Pumpkins

I had a good week with Gil at Bermuda High. Beyond the flying, it was a lot of one-to-one time, a precious commodity with a college son attending school away from home. We slept in a tent on the field, spending our evenings at the library of the University of South Carolina branch in nearby Lancaster, where I read soaring technical manuals and Gil studied Chinese. We ate a lot of Mexican food at what Gager assured us was the best local restaurant.

Gil was there to fly, too, and he was a much better student pilot than I was. By the end of my flights on the first morning I was distinctly queasy, and I fought airsickness the whole week, heightening my overall anxiety. Gil was neither sick nor anxious and just seemed more dexterous in the cockpit with the controls. He was eager to ascribe this to his hours of computer game play, but I was skeptical.

Whatever my comparative accomplishment, I ended the week in a high state. I was really and truly flying gliders, or one glider anyway, Bermuda High's workhorse training glider. It certainly wasn't ecstatic, but I was getting around up in the air without an engine. I knew it wouldn't be easy coming back to Bermuda High—an eight-hour drive from my home in central Kentucky, over the Cumberland Mountains and through the Asheville Gorge to South Carolina—but that was just a logistical problem. Far more important was that I had overcome the psychological issue: 30 years of wishing. I was convinced I could get a pilot's license at Bermuda High. It would be limited to gliders, but that was no problem either. Gliders were all I wanted to fly.

Still…eight hours was eight hours. What happened after I got my glider pilot's license? Was I going to have to go back regularly to Bermuda High to fly? There was a county airport 15 minutes from my home. I had never heard anything about gliders being flown from there, but it seemed obvious I should make an exploratory visit.

The Madison County Airport manager made it immediately clear he was not interested in my recent experiences or aspirations. He told me he knew of a glider group that flew from an airport about a two-hour drive away. That was all he knew about gliders, and all he cared to know. A speech I had practiced about my willingness to finance a local pilot to obtain tow-pilot certification and to have a tow hook installed on a suitable airplane was brushed off. "Nobody here cares about gliders," the airport manager told me. "No point in you asking around."

It was a depressing conversation. Still, after all the time I had been waiting, I was determined to go forward. I had started at Bermuda High and I would continue, hoping I would discover new options in the process. I made reservations to go back by myself for seven days in October.

For this foray I reserved "the bunkhouse," a single room off the main clubhouse with a pale pine bunk bed, a bathroom, a table, and a microwave. Living there, I was in the center of action of the gliderport. For that matter I was the center of action of the gliderport. Jim Gager was the only full-time flight instructor there, and Jayne Reid flew the tow plane. Husband Frank collaborated closely on customizing the teaching syllabus to my progress as we went along.

A glider training flight usually lasts only about 15 minutes, so there is a lot of shuffling to do. After a landing, Gager and I would pull back the bent-wire canopy latches, raise and tilt our canopies over on their side hinges, release our seat belts and clamber over the side of the sailplane. We would have a mini-conference, talking about the flight past and planning the next one. Gager would retrieve the golf cart and we would bump off with the glider back to the end of the field to position for the next tow. Jayne would be sitting in the tow plane doing office work—talking business on the cell phone with Frank or various customers and suppliers, a note pad on her knee. I would clamber back into the glider and reengage with the belts. Jayne would start up the tow plane, come swooping and roaring around with the tow rope. Gager would hook us up and give Jayne hand signals while she took out the slack. He would then perform his customary levitation into the back seat and I would go through the pre-takeoff check list: altimeter set, belt tight, my canopy down and latched, controls free, trim neutral, cable release locked, dive brakes shut. When we were ready, Gager would windmill his arm outside his open canopy to tell Jayne to go. He would fasten things quickly while she brought the towline to full tension.

With no wing runner, we had to start with a wingtip on the ground, or at least on the springy wingtip wire. When Jayne felt the line taut she would feed in the throttle, the engine would roar, the maelstrom of sand, dust, twigs, and grass clippings would blow back at us, and we would roll. Gager would bring the wingtip off the ground with hard aileron, level out, hand the glider over to me, and off our little parade would go again.

After about five morning flights we would break for lunch. Jayne would go immediately to work behind the desk. I don't know when or what she ate. I had made a peanut butter sandwich in the early hours of the morning in the bunkhouse. Gager always had some kind of strong-smelling soup he brought in an unmarked plastic container.

During lunch we would visit with the three full-time residents of the clubhouse. One was an English mastiff, simply the largest dog I had ever seen. I commented immediately that I now knew for the first time what Sherlock Holmes had felt on the heath when he came face to face with the Hound of the Baskervilles. Jayne assured me this was the gentlest dog imaginable. In fact it was clearly second fiddle to the second dog of the premises—fleet, black and white and Irish setter-shaped. "That's the one to watch," advised Jayne. I didn't know what to watch for, but I guarded my peanut butter sandwiches.

The third resident of the office suite was a large, green-bodied Amazon parrot, who occupied a tall perch in a corner. The parrot had amazing indigo and orange feathers on the underside of its wings, which it periodically exposed in indolent stretches. But it was mostly distinguished by its vocabulary, a collection of sharp retorts it had undoubtedly picked up from excited conversations in the clubhouse. It would sit fussily idle for hours without a word, entirely unprovokable, then spontaneously erupt with a string of pithy remarks, sounding for all the world like a cranky, precocious child. It also called the dogs, with an ear-splitting version of Frank's whistle. The sleeping dogs would leap awake to assess the situation, and not seeing Frank, curl back around and lie down. This would all be repeated in 15 minutes. Neither the parrot nor the dogs seemed ever to tire of the drill.

Gager and Frank would consult over my progress of the morning, planning the afternoon's flights. I would read desultorily in the Soaring Flight Manual until Gager was ready, then—usually a little too soon for me—we would go again to the golf cart.

"I'll be there when you're ready," Jayne would call out from behind her desk, paper or phone in hand. She always was.

The Incident came about mid-week. I was making progress in the air and on the ground, where activities were getting very familiar. I could vault to my seat over the side of the glider. I had solved the puzzle of the seat belts. I was dexterous in hooking and unhooking the tow cable. I could do the pre-take-off check list in my sleep. It was also getting hotter by the day, Indian summer heat. The cockpit of the glider was an efficient greenhouse, and in the minute or so after I latched my canopy, while Jayne was taking the slack out of the towline, I would get very hot indeed. If there was any holdup in procedure Gager would too.

So it was that on one such slack-taking holdup, on the last flight before lunch, Gager announced that he was cracking his canopy open and suggested I do the same. I pulled my wire latch back and cocked the canopy up with my hand. We sat for a minute until Jayne solved her problem, then Gager said, "OK, close your canopy." I let it bonk down and latched it and I heard Gager do the same. The towplane roared, the mini-maelstrom blew, I brought the glider level as we rolled—I was doing this now myself—and off we went.

The tow, heading for 2000 feet, was perfectly normal until about 1500 feet. There was a little turbulence, but not much. I was flying comfortably behind the tow plane. Then came a sprightly down gust. All at once an avalanche of wind was tearing at my face. My hat departed. I slapped at it with my non-stick hand then transferred my attention to my dark glasses as they threatened to follow. What had happened?!

The canopy! My canopy had blown open. I looked up and it was wavering overhead, held half up by the air flow. I let go my glasses and reached up for the edge to pull it down.

"FLY THE AIRPLANE," came a bellowed command from the back seat. I looked quickly for the tow plane and couldn't find it anywhere. Where was it? It had to be at the other end of the bright yellow tow line, but that was pointed almost straight down. Sure enough, in formation down below us I saw the tow plane. We were way out of position above it.

I knew—I don't know how I managed to think of this since we had never practiced any remotely similar maneuver—I knew I couldn't just dive down. My increase in speed would create dangerous slack in the line. I had to eke my way down, canting the glider a little sideways to slow it down. So I put the stick forward slightly and to the right, eased in a bit of left rudder, and we began a careful descent to the tow plane. This had all taken perhaps five seconds.

Behind me, Gager had released his seat belt and now raised himself up sufficiently to grab the edge of my canopy and pull it down. "Latch it good," he ordered. I transferred my attention from my careful flying just enough to ram the latch home.

"I have your hat," Gager said.

Gradually we sank level with the tow plane. "Good job of regaining position," offered Gager. I released breath I didn't realize I had been holding and slumped a little. "We'll talk about this when we get down. For now let's just take it up to 2000." After a pause, "Frank will probably want to talk about it too." For the rest of the flight, as we went through comfortably routine maneuvers, I thought about the talk we would have when we got down. Clearly the problem had been caused by my not fully latching my canopy after we had opened up to cool off. I kept glancing down at the latch to see how I could have made that mistake. On the other hand, I thought I had flown the glider pretty well after the canopy came open, getting back into position and all. Still…how had we gotten so far out of position? I figured that when I reached for my hat or for the canopy edge I must have sat up high in the seat, pulling the stick back when I did so. It didn't take much back pressure on the stick to make the glider zoom up on tow. I knew that the glider in a high position is very dangerous for the tow plane. The glider pulls the tow plane's tail up, causing it to dive. Close to the ground this can create huge problems. But we were 1500 feet up. Tow rules stipulate that the glider should always release when it gets so far out of position that it can't see the tow plane. We were not quite that far above. Still, the tow pilot is supposed to release if the glider gets outside a visual box behind it. I knew we were outside that box. Jayne could have released us, leaving us to deal with the 250-foot tow rope dangling from the nose of the glider.

Gager could have ordered me to release. Neither did. Instead, Gager let me fly the glider back into position. Jayne continued the tow. There were clearly positives and negatives to the situation. It surely had been good emergency practice.

So what was going to happen on the ground? Would I get yelled at by Gager? Would Gager get yelled at by Jayne? Would we all get yelled at by Frank?

As it happened, nobody yelled at anybody, though the last possibility was closest. After we landed, Jayne came over in the tow plane to be sure we were breaking for lunch. She shut down and opened her own canopy as we crawled out.

"What happened up there?" she asked in a normal tone.

"Front canopy came open," said Gager, succinctly.

"I came close to releasing you," she responded.

"Yep," said Gager. He strode off toward the golf cart. Jayne started up and bounced off to the hangar.

Nobody mentioned the incident during the desultory lunch conversation. Nobody mentioned it all afternoon. On the last flight of the day Gager and I landed long, as was the custom. This meant an extended ground-skimming coast of the glider half-way down the runway, with spoilers in. The idea was to get the glider close to the hangar under its own steam, so it could be put up easily. I enjoyed the skimming sensation about as much as any in the flying repertoire. The glider just seemed to float forever, bare inches off the ground. I was walking back to the bunkhouse with images of skimming competing with thoughts of my frozen dinner and the microwave when Frank came up. "I'd like you to join Gager and me on the porch," he said.

Frank was very matter-of-fact. He had reviewed the chain of events separately with Jayne and with Gager, getting each of their perspectives. Now it was time to turn it into a teachable moment with me, the student pilot.

I was a little surprised to learn that Gager had been doing a quick, visual, "rolling checklist" on each flight. The two chief components were "spoilers-in" and "canopies-latched." Gager had failed to notice that my canopy was not fully latched. His failure, though, both he and Frank agreed, was mitigated by the fact that I had indeed pushed the latch forward. It just hadn't gone all the way into its slot. In the future, I would be doing my own rolling checklists, Frank said. "Remember this property of the latch," he said.

Years later, I would have reason to recall this lesson.

When the canopy blew open I had done what anyone, even a seasoned pilot, would likely have done—reached for something. I had reached for my hat, then my glasses, finally the canopy itself. Such reaching absolutely always results, Frank emphasized, in pulling back on the stick. At the relatively high speed of the tow, the glider zooms up, pulling the tail of the towplane with it. Frank narrated a horrific recent incident from another soaring operation in which a tow pilot was killed and a student pilot and instructor severely injured when a canopy opened right at the beginning of a tow, close to the ground. The glider went up; the tow plane went down. No one reacted fast enough. Disaster. Our incident had occurred at 1500 feet, and therein lay the bones of confusion. Gager was convinced there had never been any danger to us or Jayne. He had acted accordingly. Jayne had not known what was happening, but was willing to give the glider the benefit of the doubt, and had not released immediately. Both right judgments, as it happened.

But Frank was not pleased. From his perspective as co-owner of a flight training school, he wanted to operate with policies that would absolutely insure safety. Such a policy in this case would have required us in the glider to release as soon as we got out of shape, and Jayne to release right away if we didn't. No judgments. No hesitation. In the future, Frank emphasized to me, and to Gager, that was what would happen. Case closed. We all shook hands. It was dinnertime.

October 31 fell on Saturday of my week at Bermuda High. In the morning, Gager announced that we would be finishing our flying earlier in the afternoon than usual. "Field activities," was all he would volunteer.

As we executed our round robin of training flights in the early afternoon, I saw cars trickling in to the airfield. By 4 p.m. there were a dozen. What was going on? Everybody seemed to know but me.

By 5 p.m. the two training gliders were staged one behind the other at the take-off end of the field. A second tow plane had been mobilized. It looked to me like a mini-contest grid. But what kind of contest could be flown at five in the afternoon?

Halfway down the runway, well out in front of the clubhouse, two guys were walking around bent over, squirting white spray paint from cans. They seemed to be creating a big square. Could it be a target? I began to get an idea. Sure enough, a few minutes later Frank called everyone together in the clubhouse for a "pilots' meeting." He raised a bulky copy of the Federal Aviation Regulations so all could see it.

"Gentlemen…and Jayne, I give you Part 91, Section 91.15," he intoned, "on Dropping of Objects."

> No pilot in command of a civil aircraft may allow any object to be dropped from that aircraft in flight that creates a hazard to persons or property. However, this section does not prohibit the dropping of any object if reasonable precautions are taken to avoid injury or damage to persons or property.

"We have taken reasonable precautions by putting the target well away from structures," Frank said. "That would be the club house and hangars.

We have even moved the fuel truck, which though far removed from what I would consider normal operations, suffered a near miss last year." (Chuckles all around.) "This is not a contest. There are no prizes. But we do have some special pilots."

At that cue the bathroom door off in one corner of the clubhouse opened and two costumed figures marched majestically toward the group. One was Batman, his ears sticking way up from his mask and his scalloped black cape flowing. The other was Superman, a little paunchy in his tight blue suit with its big red S, but with an equally impressive cape.

They were really good costumes. I was amazed. All the bystanders laughed a good deal, all the more merrily since they knew the protagonists.

Without further discussion, costumed pilots and accompanying crew members strode out the door and into golf carts, which bumped incongruously down the field toward the gliders, capes fluttering behind. Jayne and another tow pilot climbed into another cart and followed.

The rest of us ambled down the side of the field to spectate. The caped crusaders climbed into the front seats of the training gliders, their co-pilots into the rears. Canopies were lowered with bold thumbs-up gestures to the audience. The front tow plane roared and bounced into position and soon the first glider was aloft. The second followed close behind.

The gliders released low, at about 1000 feet. The first glider began a high landing approach, proceeding slowly down the side of the field, turning a square base leg well beyond the field's end, then, instead of extending spoilers and descending to the field as in a normal landing pattern, it sped up in a shallow dive. For a training glider at 500 feet, even a dive looks pretty slow, but the glider was clearly making a "high speed pass" down the field. I didn't know exactly what to look for, but as the glider neared the target area, what looked liked an orange basketball tumbled out from the front cockpit area and plummeted toward the ground. A blue arm waved. The little group of bystanders hooted.

I didn't know what to concentrate on. I was mostly watching the glider, thinking what Superman must be experiencing with his canopy open, but out of the corner of my eye I saw the orange sphere near the ground and simply disappear. I heard a small muffled thud.

A pumpkin! He had dropped a pumpkin.

Gager ran out toward the sprayed square in the middle of the field, to see where the pumpkin had hit, I guessed. I followed at a distance. There was an orange, smeared area about ten yards past the painted square and small pieces of pumpkin shrapnel scattered past that.

I looked up. The first glider had pulled into a real landing pattern. The second was entering its high speed run. I realized I really did want a closer look at the next pumpkin strike. It was not the kind of phenomenon likely to be repeated very often in my life.

Following Gager well off to the side of the square, I focused on the front cockpit of the glider. Sure enough, I saw it crack open, saw a much larger basketball than the first one rolled up on the sill, an akimbo of black arms, and then down it came. Gager and I stepped forward when it became clear where it was going to hit and were no more than ten yards away when it did.

What I saw could best be described as an orange explosion. With a clear thump the pumpkin disappeared in an orange haze. I got a dash of wet, vegetable breeze. Pieces of pumpkin tumbled down the field.

Then all was still.

Gager trotted out and ascertained that this pumpkin had indeed detonated inside the sprayed square. He turned toward the bystanders, now standing in front of the clubhouse, and put up his arms like a football referee signaling a touchdown. The group whistled and clapped.

I glanced around at the mess. "Do we need to pick up any of these pieces?" I asked him.

"Naah," said Gager. "The raccoons and possums will clean it all up tonight, though they might be a little noisy doing it. It'll be a little Halloween present for them."

At the beginning of the week there had been discussion of whether I would be able to fly by myself—to solo—by the end. I was close, but not quite there yet, by all our judgments. For my last day I could just continue what I had been doing, progressing closer to solo. But that was not what I wanted. I wanted to get a sense of what real cross-country soaring was like. Besides two training gliders—venerable tube-and-fabric American gliders designed in the 1960s—Bermuda High had a medium-high-performance two place German fiberglass glider. I wanted to rent the higher performance glider and have Gager take me out in the country away from the airfield. I hoped for two or three hours of flying, returning to the main field for a final triumphant landing.

It was not to be. Gager went over the weather forecast in the morning with me: stable air, with enough of an overcast to cut off most thermal development. Still, we could fly the higher performance glider so I could get a feel for it.

In all my years of attending soaring events I had never been in a situation in which I could look close-up at a modern glider. Now, going over the German glider in a pre-flight examination, I was able to do that. Of course the overall lines were much sleeker than the old American glider, but the two things that impressed me most were the incredible slickness of the finish on the fiberglass and the efforts made to reduce the turbulence of air flowing over the surfaces and the resultant drag. The finish was sufficiently slick that I could see my face reflected in it at close range. And everywhere surfaces joined the joints were taped, while components thrust out into the air flow—like wheels—were enclosed in fiberglass fairings. All this made it possible for the glider to fly as fast as 175 miles an hour, and to fly forward 34 feet for each foot it dropped. By contrast, the American training glider's top speed was 98 miles per hour, and its glide ratio about 22.

I knew all this intellectually, but I didn't appreciate what it would mean for flying characteristics. The difference was notable as soon as the Gager turned the glider over to me on tow. I was struck by an automotive analogy. The American training glider felt like the kind of big, 20-year-old Ford or Chevy my father drove. Everything was loud and loose; every control had play in it. The German glider by contrast felt like a Jaguar sedan—silent, tight, smooth. One motion of the glider flowed sinuously into another, and the visibility through the over-the-top canopy was amazing, almost like no canopy at all.

I was able to climb in a few small thermals and put the glider through its paces, staying within gliding distance of the airport. It wasn't ecstatic flying, but I was fairly thrilled; this was closer to what I had been expecting. Weather rules soaring, though, and after about 45 minutes the overcast thickened and the air died. We returned to the airport and Gager flew the landing.

I knew I wanted more of that kind of flying.

The Hills

It's a year later, 1999. I am eating breakfast in my car. It's the pale, half-light of a 6:30 a.m. north-Georgia-November dawn. I'm parked in a rutted, cleared area at the end of a twisty gravel road, staring over the steering wheel into the woods.

I'm parked here waiting to go hang gliding.

My breakfast is a milky bowl of Cheerios into which I have cut wedges of a crisp Granny Smith apple. On the passenger seat next to me stand quart cartons of milk and orange juice. Every so often, between spoonfuls of Cheerios and apple, I reach for one or the other and take a swig.

I was assured last night in the operations building of the Lookout Mountain Flight Park that instructors would appear by 7 a.m. Now, though, it is totally still. The only sign of civilization is a rusted, cabless, semi-trailer, its rear door facing out toward me in the parking area, its front disappearing into the woods. I munch, swig, and stare.

I have come to this clearing at the northwestern tip of Georgia on the advice of my younger son, Gil. It's a convoluted story.

After the spring-break trip to the Bermuda High Soaring School with Gil the previous year and my subsequent adventures there in the fall, he and I had planned to spend his sophomore year spring break at Bermuda High again, hoping we would both solo. But in early February when I got around to calling, Bermuda High was booked.

"I'm sure sorry," Jayne said. "I know you and Gil were planning to come back. But I got a really early booking for three students for that week, and you know we can only handle two or three full-time students at a time."

It was disappointing. I had put a lot of physical and psychological energy into getting comfortable with the aircraft, the people, and the protocols at Bermuda High. I was also looking forward intensely to more flying in the German fiberglass glider. But if Gil and I were to share another glider flying experience, it would have to be somewhere else.

The only other commercial glider operation I knew of in our part of the country was the Chilhowee Gliderport, down I-75 between Knoxville and Chattanooga, three hours south of our home in Kentucky. Our family had visited the place when we lived in Knoxville, but I hadn't gone back. I knew from *Soaring* magazine that the gliderport had been established in the early 1970s by a free-spirited educator named Mike Reisman. I also knew that Reisman had died shortly before in a kayaking accident. I didn't know whether the glider operation was continuing or not.

Mike Reisman's son Will answered the phone at the gliderport. He said he was taking a year off between college and medical school to keep the business afloat, with financial and logistical support from a group of soaring enthusiasts who valued the operation. He took my reservation for four days in March, but he wouldn't be able to tell me who our instructor or tow pilot would be, only that there would be one each day.

He did remind me though, of the 1100-foot tall ridge of the Appalachian Mountains that ran alongside the field 20 miles southwest to northeast. A wind blowing hard from the northwest would sweep up the whole length of the ridge and could maintain a Glider all day long, just cruising up and back. Such winds were common in March, Reisman assured me.

Gil and I hustled down the interstate on the first afternoon of his spring break, down to Benton, Tennessee, the nearest town to the Chilhowee Gliderport. We booked a faintly seedy motel for four nights. Out at the gliderport in the morning, Will Reisman was working on the brakes of the tow-plane, a reconditioned WWII spotter in full military paint. Will introduced us to Ray, our flight instructor, a stocky fellow somewhere between Gil's and my ages, packing a hand-held radio and a battery-operated tape recorder. Will pronounced the tow plane brakes serviceable, and we all moved to extract the teaching glider—an all-metal number designed and manufactured in Czechoslovakia—from the hangar.

Under a benign sky, that first day was spent in the cycle of tows and 15-minute up-and-down flights Gil and I knew so well from Bermuda High. The weather changed overnight though, and we were greeted at the gliderport the next morning by a northwest wind I regarded as beyond brisk. Ray was unfazed, and shortly I was in the front seat of the sailplane working to keep the wings level as the tow plane, piloted by Will, bounced down the field. We weren't 50 feet in the air when the first gust hit, and after that it was like trying to follow a deranged boomerang around the sky. The tow plane zoomed, dived, and rolled, and I followed in a kind of survival mode, flailing the controls far harder than I had ever done at Bermuda High, convinced I was doing just an appallingly bad job. Several times I was sure Will would release us; several times I thought we should release ourselves. But every time I expostulated, Ray just said, "Hang on. We'll be through this soon."

He was right. Above the ridge the air smoothed out considerably. "OK," said Ray. "Up air the rest of the way. I'll call down and tell Will to put up the tow plane, tell Gil to go sit inside. We'll be up as long as we want." He explained that we had towed through the "rotor," the curlicued turbulence of air cascading down the lee side of the ridge. Just our bad luck the rotor was right over the glider field just then. But I had done very well with the tow, Ray said, given the conditions.

Flying the ridge lift was exciting. I could put the nose down and fly along the treetops almost as fast as the glider could go, buoyed up by the ever-up-sweeping air. I could zoom up, wingover back down, fly figure-eights against the hillside. We stayed up for almost three hours, flying the whole length of the ridge several times, practicing sequences of maneuvers that would have been impossible on typical short training flights. I felt wrung out but exhilarated when we finally landed.

In the clubhouse eating lunch before taking off with Gil, Ray produced from his coat pocket a cassette tape. I remembered the tape recorder from the first day. "I tape parts of a training flight that might be valuable to think about," he said. "In this case, I taped the tow through the rotor." He looked over at Will and smiled. "Roger might be surprised at some of the language he used while we were getting bounced around up there."

Gil and I had a lot to talk about that evening at dinner, both looking forward to a third day of flying, though the forecast was not encouraging. Sure enough, we woke up to fog and rain. We drove over to the gliderport, but Will was sure the wet conditions would last the next several days. We were still exhilarated from the ridge flying, but were disappointed there was not more of any other kind. It looked like our flying for the trip was over.

We just couldn't bear to go back to Kentucky right away, so we decided to spend the day in Chattanooga. We drove in to visit the magnificent aquarium there, then spent some time in the public library. Late in the rainy afternoon we decided to drive up to the top of Lookout Mountain.

I had read about the Lookout Mountain Flight Park, one of the premier hang gliding sites in the east, but it had never occurred to me to visit. I had never had any interest in hang gliding. It seemed a way-too-risky business for me, hanging out in the breeze under a Dacron sail. But Gil and I had time to kill, another night to spend, and unrequited visions of flying on our minds. It seemed worth a drive up the mountain on pure curiosity.

We passed out of Chattanooga proper and began climbing up through suburban-esque neighborhoods in ever-denser rainy fog. We passed the entrance to Rock City, the labyrinthine mountaintop site widely advertised with red-roofed black birdhouses beside back roads all over the southeast. We passed mansions built at the turn of the century by wealthy Atlantans looking for respite from the summer heat, great hulks of houses looking all the more prepossessing in the fog. Nearing the top of the ridge we passed Covenant College, the most recent incarnation of what had been a huge hotel in the Roaring Twenties. I had heard in my youth from my Baptist elders, as we passed in the valley below Covenant's mountaintop tower silhouette, that the building had been a speakeasy and bordello during the Depression. Finally, down the narrowest spine of the ridge in the now decidedly spooky deep fog, we came to a two-story aluminum frame building, the headquarters of the Flight Park.

On such a day, not much was happening inside. But Matt Taber, the eloquent and charismatic creator of the LMFP, was there, and he soon had us enthralled by the prospect of hang gliding. Why, right that minute, said Matt, 2000 feet below us in the landing area of the flight park, on the other side of the ridge from Chattanooga, conditions were calm and nicely flyable. Why not try an introductory hop? A two-place hang glider and instructor were available. A tow plane would tow it up just as it did a sailplane. As sailplane pilots we would have no problem with any of it.

Gil was game. I was delighted to have a teenage son willing to try things out. So down the mountain we went.

At the bottom of the ridge, at one end of the 2600-foot landing area, we met Mike, the tandem glider instructor. He was lazing in a wooden gazebo, its walls festooned with big canvas vests from which hung spider webs of straps. A row of helmets ran along a bench. Beside the gazebo was cocked a truly vast green and red hang glider and beside it a gangly pale-yellow ultralight airplane, its engine mounted nakedly behind its single high wing, the propeller pointing backwards. Mike greeted us enthusiastically and sized Gil for a vest and helmet, buckling all the vest straps to make it into a hang glider harness. With a grand gesture he stepped off the porch of the gazebo and beckoned Gil to the glider: "Let's step into my office."

While Mike was putting on his own full-suited harness and getting them both hooked up to the glider, a four-wheeler came bouncing and bucking across the field. It careened to a halt next to the gazebo and a t-shirted young man leaped off it, waved in our direction, and crawled immediately into the ultralight's seat. In barely a moment the engine was crackling and the towplane jouncing forward, towline slack disappearing in the process. Mike gave a casual wave, and without even pausing, the towplane surged forward with the glider in tow. It was just like a sailplane operation, but ever-so-much quicker and more informal.

I stood beside the gazebo, my arms folded, looking up. The tow was the same kind of graceful pas de deux as a sailplane tow, though appearing almost to stand still as the pair gained altitude. When the now-tiny green-red delta finally detached from the tow plane above the ridge, it looked to me as though it were hanging in the air, and it did so for what seemed like minutes before beginning a series of slow figure-eights. I got distracted watching the tow plane spinning deliriously back to the field and then by other hang gliders being carried like giant bright butterflies on pilots' shoulders. Looking after an interval back up the ridge for the two-place glider, I was surprised to hear Gil's voice, speaking in normal tones, coming out of the silence somewhere above my head. A lower-pitched voice replied to him. They were talking about spring leaf color.

Craning up and around, I was taken aback to see the big wing 500 feet above, flying a lazy circle. Gil and Mike were hanging below it, pointing and enjoying a casual conversation. This certainly looked like a relaxed way of flying. The two conversationalists and the glider finally made their way to the other end of the field, executed a swooping u-turn, settled into a grass-skimming approach, and rolled to a stop 20 yards in front of me. Gil and Mike stood up and unbuckled their harnesses, and Gil walked thoughtfully over to me. We watched Mike amble out to talk to one of the pilots now hooking up for a tow.

Gil turned and said, "Dad, I think this might be what you have been looking for."

After we got back to Kentucky I thought long and hard about Gil's diagnosis. We had talked a good deal on our drive back. Hang gliding truly could be what I was looking for in flying. It was also way less aircraft and airport intensive—and way cheaper—than the world of sailplanes. It seemed to me I should try it.

So here I am, about to take my first hang glider flight. I bought a five-day pre-paid package of instruction: five mornings of foot-launch instruction on "the hills," and five tandem towed flights from the LZ, the "landing zone" at the base of Missionary Ridge. I have received a brief ground school course on foot launching in which I have learned that I will run down a grassy hill and the wing will lift me effortlessly as I run. I have seen a video. It looks straightforward. I can see one grassy hill from where I sit in the car. It's a misty 200 yards away off to my right, beyond the edges of my clearing. It looks odd, a large bump with a tiny orange wind sock on top, in the dead middle of a winter-yellow field. It looks higher than the hill in the video. I wonder idly how the gliders get out to and up the hill.

A white rental car sidles up beside me. The driver is eating a sweet roll half out of a plastic wrapper. He drinks coffee from a steaming styrofoam cup. He doesn't look at me. While I am covertly glancing at him, a dusty black pick-up truck bounces from behind us into the clearing. A rectangular rack frame sprouts from the back of the bed. A rack bar stretches across the cab top, and T-bars rear up from the front bumper. Two fat hang glider bags are tied onto this assemblage. It is 7:05 a.m. The instructors have arrived.

Two 20-something guys bound out of the truck. One heads to the back of the semi trailer. The other strides over and passes around the backs of our cars, knocking on rear windows.

"Rise and shine, guys," he carols. "It's time to go hang gliding." He heads past us into the edge of the woods to take a pee.

The driver next door and I emerge from our cars and shuffle with our hands in our pockets toward the trailer. A third car pulls into the clearing.

The back of the trailer is now open and the first instructor has disappeared inside. I glance in and see a mangle of harnesses hanging to the right of the door, a pile of variously colored helmets on the floor beneath them like so many discarded skulls, and past them, in parallel rows pointing into the dim recesses of the trailer, hang glider bags suspended on each side of the trailer. These are long, thin, bags, really long bags, eighteen-foot-long bags. Two sets of four per side, two sides…that's 16 hang gliders in this trailer. That's a bunch.

It looks like we are only three students.

The first instructor materializes from the back of the trailer. The second trots up behind us. It's time for introductions.

The instructors introduce each other, then us. They have clearly read our rap sheets. Everyone gets a first name and couple of significant details. Frank, the instructor from inside the trailer, is soft-spoken. He's thin and a little owlish, with trim black hair and glasses. Ron is stocky, blond and tousled, ebullient. Ron tells us that Frank was a biology teacher at the high school in nearby Trenton, Georgia. He came over to the flight park to see what was going on. Now he is a Hang-3-rated pilot and a full-time instructor. No more biology teaching. Frank tells us that Ron is from Florida, where he works in the winter on charter fishing boats. He too is a Hang-3 and a three-season instructor at Lookout. My next-car mate is Bill, from Houston. He already knows how to hang glide, having learned at a tow-only operation there in "the flatlands." He has flown commercially all the way to Lookout Mountain to learn to foot launch, to run off mountains. This is his second trip up. Terry, who arrived last, is from Georgetown, Kentucky, near where I live. He is an engineer at the giant Toyota plant there. I am "the professor," a re-treading sailplane pilot. I wish.

Frank demonstrates the harnesses, which look like baseball catchers' chest protectors with extra straps in the back. He comments on their gamey smell. When I am handed one, I see immediately what he means. He flings out helmets to try for size. He compliments Terry on wearing knee pads with his shorts. Knee pads?

While Frank has been dispensing harnesses and helmets, Ron has been poking around back in the trailer, reading numbers written in wide, black magic marker ink on the ends of the glider bags. Now he comes out beside Frank.

"What do you weigh, Roger?"

I tell him about 160 pounds.

"We'll put you in a 146. You're right on the cusp. But the smaller glider will be easier to handle, and flying faster will be good for you."

I'm not sure what any of this means. But Terry and Bill are both heavier than I am and they get "164s."

"Come on up," says Ron, and we plod single file up the ramp into the narrow center aisle of the trailer, between the rows of glider bags. Ron points me to a gray bag with red ends. I see "146" scrawled on the end nearest me. The bags, I see, are all suspended on metal arms, three for each bag, emerging from a rack system along the walls of the trailer. I reach under the bag and lift it. It is not terribly heavy, but how to carry it? I see Ron with a bag on his shoulder striding easily down the trailer ramp. I swing my bag up to my shoulder awkwardly, turn slightly, and immediately bang the rear end behind me. Nine feet long fore and aft, the bag is astoundingly clumsy to handle. It seems impossible to walk it in a straight line.

Still, clumsy or not, bags lifted and banged, calls to "Duck!" uttered usually after the fact, eventually we three students and Ron all stand beside our bags, harnesses, and helmets at the edge of the field, facing out toward the Hill. From this perspective I see that to the extreme left end of the field is another hill, much taller, really a shelf, merging into a hillside that moves up far beyond the parking clearing. Ron has unzipped his bag from end to end and is reaching into it. He will demonstrate assembly with one glider. Frank will move among us and help us emulate Ron.

Ron assembles an aluminum triangle from the middle of the bag, adds big, black, hollow plastic wheels on either corner. He stoops over, reaches under the bag, pivots it on one of the corner wheels and flips it up to stand on both, one bag end on the ground. Now the bag comes off and he spreads the wings, a mass of red Dacron unfurling and hanging slack from the V-formed leading edge. Battens like those on a sailboat sail go into hidden slots from back to front in the Dacron and the airfoil takes shape. A move to the center keel of the V, a pull on a cable, and the whole wing tightens up like a drum.

It is really quite a beautiful sight.

I recall occasions on group camping trips with rented equipment when I have watched an experienced hand demonstrate the erection of an unfamiliar tent. I know it's going to be easy when I know how, but the one demonstration is not enough for me to know how. It is certainly that way here. There are fine, steel-braided wires to untangle, safety pins to put through holes in bolt bottoms, battens to size in pairs. There's the A-frame with its down and base tubes, the keel, the cross bar, king post, washout tubes and luff lines. Bill, the flatlander hang glider pilot, keeps pace with Ron as he works. Terry and I, after unzipping bags and attaching wheels to A-frames, simply stand and watch. Frank darts back and forth between us. Ron joins in after he's finished with his own glider.

And eventually—I know I will need just as much help breaking the glider down at the end of the session as I needed putting it together—there stand the four gliders on their base-tube wheels, keels, and wing tips. V-apex noses point toward the sky, taut, colorful, and very official-looking. My glider has a deep red V-section in the front with white behind. Terry's is blue and white. Bill's is chartreuse and kelly green. Ron's is a brownish red all over, like an old red sail on a ship. All four standing together are a pretty sight.

But there's no time for aesthetics. Ron has draped his harness over himself without buckling anything, stuck his helmet on backwards, stepped under the A-frame and is carrying his glider out toward the hill. Frank stays behind to instruct. We are to back, stooped, in under the A-frame, wedge our shoulders into its narrowing space at the top, grab the down tubes, and stand up. The base tube will be in front of and below our knees. We will walk carrying the 50-pound gliders like this the 200 yards out to the hill. As soon as I take the weight of the glider on my shoulders, I know what the thick padding toward the top of the down tubes is for.

It's a long carry out to the hill. Way out in front of us, Ron doesn't even pause when he gets to its base. In stride, he goes right to the top, puts the glider down, spreads his arms, and lets out a whoop. It sets a good tone. Frank walks along with us, carrying an orange and white water jug and a plastic bag of cups. It had not occurred to me that the weather might be hot.

I am hot when I get to the top of the hill. And a bit out of breath. And even with all the padding, my shoulders are sore where the glider has rested on them. Terry is about the same. One of his knee pads has slid down around his ankle. Bill is a good deal out of breath and sits down in the dust under his glider.

But Ron is ready to go. He has cinched up his harness, fastened his helmet, and is ready to demonstrate the "hang check," the last thing you do before launching yourself and your glider off the hill. Backing in under his A-frame, he twists around and looks for the hang straps, two thick, white, nylon straps looped around the keel of his glider near the cross bar, one shorter than the other. The various straps at the back of his harness are gathered into a D-shaped clamp he calls a carabiner, and he hooks this carabiner to the hang straps and screws a collar into place.

"OK baby, I'm hooked in," he chortles. "This is a hang check."

He stoops again behind the base tube. Frank pulls the nose down until it is level. Now Ron is suspended in flying position within the A-frame, his head and shoulders six or eight inches above the base.

"It's the three Cs, gentlemen," he says.

"Crotch." Ron tugs at the leg strap loops, squirms in the harness. "Check the harness to be sure your legs are through the leg loops and the crotch position is secure."

"Chest." He balls his hands into fists, bounces them sideways fist over fist from the base tube to his chest. "Three fists is about right for base bar control. Too low or too high and you won't get good leverage and extension."

"Carabiner." He twists around and looks up at the carabiner. "Double check that carabiner. Be sure the collar is screwed up where it needs to be." He draws a breath. "OK. I'm set."

Frank lowers the keel of the glider to the ground. Ron kneels and then stands up, the glider on his shoulders. He looks at the little wind sock, hanging limply in the early morning air, walks across the crest of the hill in the direction of the parking area, just to where the serious slope begins. He talks over his shoulder to us. "I'm going to grip the down tubes lightly from behind, with just my thumbs and forefingers like this, what I'm happy to call the 'beer bottle' grip."

"I'm going to level the nose" (he brings it down), "and check the left and right tips to see that the whole wing is level." He turns his head back and forth. "I'm going to pick a focus point, out a good ways, like that big tree on the edge of the field, and keep my eyes on it for the whole flight. Don't look down at the ground!"

"I'm going to start with a couple of slow steps, but pick up speed fast, and keep running right off the ground. You know how Wile E. Coyote does when he runs off a cliff, legs still spinning? That's me." He takes a breath.

"If I do all that, the glider will fly me off. I won't have to do a thing to it." He takes another breath, fixes his gaze, gathers himself, and with two steps and a rush is straight into the air, the hill dropping away beneath him. It's one of the most wonderful things I have ever seen. I have fantasized about just running off a hill or a mountain into the air like that for as long as I can remember. In that moment, I think that Gil was surely right.

We watch the back of the glider as it floats straight as an arrow out over the bottom of the hill and over the field towards the parking clearing, losing altitude slowly. Just before it gets to the ground it suddenly pitches up, stops in the air, and drops straight down, level to the ground. Ron turns around to face us, standing up straight. He has landed perfectly on his feet. Frank, imperturbable Frank, lets out a big whoop and claps wildly. Ron whoops back. We all whoop. "That, gentlemen," says Frank, "is what it's all about. Who wants to be first?"

Terry volunteers. Frank helps him tighten up his harness, hooks him in, goes through the hang check with him. Ron has walked his glider back up to the top of the hill by now. Terry shuffles to the brow. Frank will hold the keel in the back as Terry runs, to keep the nose level. Ron will run alongside, just in case. Terry breathes, fixes, gathers, and the odd trio heads off.

Everything stays level, but Terry never runs quite fast enough. Frank and Ron drop off as the hill does, and Terry keeps running down it. But as the glider gets light he trips, and slides down the last third of the hill on his stomach, with serious scraping and a trail of rolling pebbles. It looks pretty bad. Ron and Frank pelt down to the bottom. They unhook Terry, call out that he's OK, and Ron starts walking the glider back up while Frank walks with Terry, talking encouragement. The chest-protector harness and the wheels have done their jobs. Terry has no problems with his hands or front. But one knee protector is down around his ankle again, and that knee is oozing bright red.

"Bad hill burn," says Frank, as we all stand around. Terry is embarrassed. My sense of the beauty of the experience has evaporated. Frank sends Terry over to the water jug to wash off his knee. I know it is going to sting like crazy. Bill goes next, and makes a credible flight in the same direction, just staying prone and rolling on the ground to a stop at the end. He unhooks far out in the field and starts back with his glider.

So now it's my turn. I am absolutely not going to run too slowly. We move to a different direction, so as not to fly toward Bill. Looking down from this new vantage point, I suddenly feel that it's pretty steep. The bottom is pretty far down. I allow that I'm perfectly happy to wait for Bill. But no. Frank is behind me on the keel and Ron is on my right wingtip.

"Any time," says Ron.

I take one slow step and go straight to an all-out bolt. I can feel Frank pushing the nose down. I run and am dimly aware of the glider pulling at my back. Then my feet are barely brushing the surface, then they're off and…I'm flying! I look down and the ground is dropping away. It's an indescribable thrill. I'm flying! It's air past my head, and quiet, and smooth, and my legs dangling, and space below me, and…I'm really flying.

I keep looking at the ground and suddenly realize it's getting closer. Then it's getting closer fast and comes right up to meet me. My knees hit first and then I'm flat and sliding along the grass. I stop finally and everything is still.

"You OK?" I hear from the top of the hill. I realize I have been just lying there.

"Yeah. It's great!" I shout back, stumble up, and unhook. I notice that my left jean's knee is ripped open. I have a fair strawberry myself. I am really clear about kneepads now. I pick up the glider and march toward the hill. Bill is still a good ways out.

We get to the top about the same time. Bill is winded and sits down under his glider again. Terry is ready to go. I will go again as soon as I get a drink of water. The airless harness is hot and I'm sweaty inside it. It's not hard to see where their gamey smell comes from. But I'm pumped, excited about trying again.

So it goes. The three of us fly in rotation, working on specific things: keeping our feet crossed behind us instead of letting them dangle, proning out before sliding in for the landing (the standup landing will come later), keeping our eyes off the ground. After four flights each we try handling a launch by ourselves. Accidental turns ensue from unleveled wings, but nobody spins back into the hill. Terry is smoothest of us, and never says a word about his strawberried knee. Bill is about the same each time but is clearly getting really tired. I think my technique is regressing.

About 10 a.m. the air begins to move and we call it quits. Nobody is sorry to stop. Bill allows that he may have a little muscle pull. While Terry and I follow Ron's example and carry our gliders back on our shoulders, Bill tows his backwards by the keel, rolling it along on the wheels.

Ron and Frank pretty much do the packing up on all four gliders. Bill sits under a tree, drinking a Coke he has brought. Terry and I stand close, following the break-down monologues. There's a particular order of things, and a special way of folding the sails. I think it would be nice to have a handout.

We stumble the long bags back to the trailer ramp, and Ron takes them one at a time back to their places along the wall. Smelly, dusty harnesses are hung, helmets tossed in the pile. I note that mine was green. The only green one. Frank fills out paperwork.

Finally, the trailer ramp up, doors closed in the middle and locked, we gather. "All you going to be back tomorrow?" Frank queries. We are. Bill says something about his muscle pull. Ron advises a hot bath and ibuprofen.

"Ron has the day off tomorrow," says Frank. I'm disappointed. "But I'll be here, and Tony, I think." Ron and he talk briefly about who the other instructor might be.

"And there will be people on the big hill tomorrow too." I imagine that the "big hill" must be the shelf I noticed this morning, on the far left side of the field. That should be interesting.

"So," says Frank. "We'll see you at 7 a.m."

Terry and I go to lunch together, at Brock's Restaurant on the town square in Trenton: pot roast, three vegetables, roll, peach cobbler, sweet tea for $4.75. Large, dusty men in overalls and billed caps fill the tables. Two State Troopers. "What can I get you, honey?" asks the waitress, whom one of the Troopers calls Thelma.

Terry is 37. He has never had a vacation away from home in the ten years he has worked for Toyota. This is the first time he has ever traveled without his wife. What a big deal this must be for him.

I spend the night in the bunkhouse at the edge of the LZ: real bunks, men on one side, women on the other of a commons area. One bathroom with multiple sinks and stalls on either side, bring your own bedding. Talk in the commons area is all of hang gliding: ridge and LZ, blowing over the back, sled rides, whacks and rolling in. Terry is staying in the Holiday Inn in Trenton.

I am glad when everyone turns in early.

The three of us work hard the next day, flight after flight, glider-carrying trudge up the hill after glider-carrying trudge up the hill. Bill is having a pretty tough time physically. He flies once for each two times Terry and I fly. Frank offers mildly that Bill might want to arrange up at the shop for a "caddy," someone who would be paid by the hour to carry the glider around. It seems a little harsh to me, as Frank and Tony are standing around a lot. But there seems to be a strong protocol about carrying your own equipment.

Over on the big hill three gliders are working. They come off a good deal higher than we are. And they are clearly practicing turns. On one rotation all three gliders in sequence will do a single left turn before they land. Then all three will do a right turn. By late in the morning they are doing s-turns.

By late in the morning we are trying stand-up landings. We land too fast to keep our footing and fall over with the glider on its nose—a "whack" in hang gliding parlance after the sound all that aluminum and taut Dacron makes when the glider's nose hits. We push the glider up too early, stop in the air, and hold our breaths while we fall—parachute—three or four feet straight down. We land squatted when we push up too late with the glider too slow. The gliders, I think, take a lot of abuse.

We take good deal of abuse too. My shoulders were bruised and my legs were sore when I woke up this morning. My strawberried knee was tight. Terry showed up wearing long pants with his knee pads taped securely on the outside. I am drinking water on top of the hill and hoping we'll quit pretty soon when I hear Frank call out, "Are you OK?"

I look out into the field. Bill has left his glider where he landed it and is walking, limping actually, back to the parking area. Frank hurries down the hill, catches up to Bill. They walk along together for a bit, then Frank turns and comes back up.

Bill has really pulled a muscle this time, Frank tells us. He is going straight back to his motel and will try to get to Atlanta to take a flight back to Houston this afternoon. He is not very happy. The same thing happened to him, it turns out, the previous time he came to Lookout to learn to foot launch. I am thinking that his week-long instructional package is not refundable.

"With all the banging, sliding, and whacking, that's the most common injury out here," Frank says. "Pulled muscles."

The next day Terry and I fly from the big hill. Ron is back, acting as sole instructor for the more experienced students on the big hill. There are five students, including a big swarthy guy with long hair who drove up on a Harley-Davidson. He wants to start right off with s-turns. But Ron wants us all to do the same maneuver each round, so he, and we, can do careful critiques. The big guy is sulky. Ron lets him go first. He makes a steep right turn and almost plows back into the hillside. Ron goes down the hill to talk to him as he carries the glider back up.

Terry goes before me and has what I think is a splendid flight. It lasts much longer than the flights from the "bunny hill" (as it seems to be called up here), which indeed looks fairly innocuous out in the middle of the field. Terry makes a smooth launch, floats forever, and lands standing up. Ron whoops. I am a little jealous. And pretty scared of the hill. There's a runable slope for 30 feet below us, then it drops off big time. You have to be airborne by then. No one has had any trouble with it, but I have been trying hard not to think of what it would be like to fall over that drop-off with the glider.

Ron told Terry and me this morning—the only first-timers on the big hill—"Don't think about it. Just do it." But it's a strange sensation—to have to ignore my inner dialogue and images and do something strongly against part of my will. It's a rare—happily rare—experience of a truly divided self.

There's nothing philosophical about my flight, though. I run very fast, get light and am airborne all in a rush. I glance down and see the ground fall away, way away below me. It's as exhilarating as my first flight off the bunny hill! I'm way up in the air, and feeling quite thrillingly motionless.

I am vaguely conscious of a whistle blowing. Oh yes. The stall whistle. Ron had it on—an oversize, orange whistle—hanging from a lanyard around his neck this morning. He told us he would blow it if he thought any of us were in danger of stalling our gliders in flight. I have been so rapturous I have paid no attention to the glider. I pull in the base tube slightly and feel the glider pick up speed. Before I want it to I see the ground coming up. I push the bar out a little too early, hold it while the glider parachutes down, land on my feet, fall to one knee. I hear a whoop from the top of the hill. Good old Ron. What a great guy. What a great experience!

It's a steep carry back up to the top of the hill.

But I can't wait to go again.

Trikes

I am looking down on cows. Way down. 1500 feet down.

The cows are tiny, black and white. They are walking in a line toward a gate in a fence along the right side of an October-brown field. Beyond the gate a barn's roof gleams rusty silver in the late evening sun.

"Roger, I thought we had agreed to fly straight down this road."

The edge in Lucian Bartosik's British-modulated voice cuts through the whooshing from the headphones built into my helmet. My attention jerks to the road below us, which is about to turn 75 degrees left alongside the field. During the three seconds I have looked at the cows, we have drifted five degrees right, off the line of the road.

"Why aren't we doing so then?" Lucian's tone implies willful negligence.

I can feel the little knot of tension twisting in my stomach. "I was looking at cows," I mutter into the spongy golf ball mic pressed against my lips, thinking dimly that it is an honest statement. Immediately I regret saying it.

"Right. And while you were looking at cows, the airplane was flying itself." Lucian's voice goes up a notch, and I feel the tension-knot twist tighter. "One of these days your engine will quit and you'll be setting up your only possible safe landing in a field two wingspans wide. You allow a drift like that to creep in and you'll clip a tree with a wingtip, cartwheel into the ground, and die."

Lucian is my flight instructor. One of his primary teaching strategies is to instantiate errors in my flying into worst-case scenarios and describe the consequences. I would like to think this arises from a genuine concern for my welfare, but he seems to take errors in my flying as personal insults to his airmanship. This doesn't help with the pressure I am already putting on myself.

I try to keep from visualizing this latest deathly scenario as I feel for the slight right pressure on the control bar I must hold for exactly the right length of time in order to get back to straight down the road. And no sooner do I get straight than I have to begin the 75-degree left turn to follow the road's bend.

It all happens, as usual, just a little too fast for me.

The aircraft I am flying is a species defined by the FAA as "ultralight." Among ultralight aficionados, it is called a "trike." If you were positioned directly above us, watching me weave gently back and forth over this country road in rural Kentucky, you would see a big, white, hang glider wing, severely swept-back and arcing continuously along its back edge from pointed tips to a short pointed tail. Just a wing. From the cows' pasture below, you would see the swept-back front of the wing black and the arcing rear section iron-ore umber, set off by the tail that's bright red like a red-tailed hawk. But instead of pilots suspended beneath the wing in normal hang glider fashion, you would see a gondola, and Lucian's and my two white helmets in the gondola, one close behind the other.

Seen up close, the gondola Lucian and I are suspended in appears a sleek, black fiberglass shell, low and narrowly conical in front, with a tiny windshield. Behind the windshield are two seats, one directly behind the other and slightly higher, like a motorcycle. A black mast rises above the rear seat, making a triangle where it connects to the keel of the wing with a more slender mast running to the front of the gondola. Behind the main mast is an engine, propeller facing backward. The propeller has three slender fiberglass blades, trisecting the circle of their four-foot arc.

The gondola is perched on three wheels, hence the appellation "trike." The rear wheels reach out on either side under the engine. They are enclosed in black fiberglass teardrops. The nose wheel is within the conical front of the gondola.

The FAA doesn't require flight instruction in "ultralight vehicles" (as distinguished from "aircraft"). If the vehicle is light enough, carries only one person and only a small amount of fuel, and flies slowly enough, no FAA certification of either the pilot or flying machine is required. Not having to deal with the FAA was a big impetus in the growth of the ultralight movement. Informally, received wisdom in the field was that the FAA was willing to pass on regulation since accidents in ultralights were likely to kill only the pilot. Unfortunately, in the early days of hang gliders and powered ultralights, many would-be pilots were killed teaching themselves to fly.

The United States Ultralight Association (now the United States Hang Glider and Paraglider Association) stepped into the vacuum left by the FAA, with instructor certification and instructional guidelines. Now two-place trainers—too heavy technically to be ultralights—operate under a waiver from the FAA. Lucian's trike is one such, bearing a big sign on the side: For Instructional Purposes Only.

At the end of my first prepaid five days the previous summer at Lookout Mountain, my efforts from the big hill with Ron and Frank and in the towed tandem glider with Mike were coming together nicely. I could foot launch confidently from the big hill, fly a sinuous pattern of s-turns across the field, and land standing up. In the tandem glider with Mike, I handled the tows with aplomb, figure-eighted symmetrically against the mountainside, climbed in thermals, and rolled-in my landings smoothly in the LZ. Every flight was thrilling. Libby said on the telephone she had not known me to be so euphoric about anything since the birth of our first child. We had a talk about the future of my flying, and on the day before my last day, I bought a hang glider wing, brand new, from Matt Taber.

On my last morning on the hills Ron helped me assemble the new wing for the first time, half a dozen other students looking on in what I took to be shades of bemusement and jealousy. The wing was bright, crisp, and shiny out of the bag, a band of profound red at the front, blue behind the red, white to the rear. Its capability was categorized as Intermediate, with a control to adjust sail tension—and gliding capability—in flight. Among the teaching gliders it stood out like a newly unfurled butterfly, the others ragged and forlorn by comparison. Ron would fly it first, to be sure it was rigged to fly straight and true.

At the top of the bunny hill Ron took a moment to explain to the group the structural features that distinguished this state-of-the-art Intermediate glider from the basic teaching models, a bit of salesmanship, it seemed to me. I stood aside in a mixture of pride and embarrassment while he hooked in, performed his hang check, stood up, and prepared to launch.

"Look for it to go 20 or 30 yards further than you're used to," he said to the group.

It didn't. It began veering right as soon as it was airborne, and despite what were clearly energetic inputs to the control bar from Ron, it continued in a series of right-bending arcs across the field, ending in a tip-dragging whack.

"No harm done," called Ron when he had unhooked and stood up. None to the glider, perhaps, but my expectations had surely taken a hit.

"Some kind of rigging issue," Ron mumbled, as we trudged with the glider back to the assembly area. "We'll get it sorted out. You're coming back, right? It'll be perfect when you're ready to fly it."

Back in the headquarters building, Matt was apologetic. Of course it was a rigging issue, and their problem, since the glider frame components and sails were shipped to them separately and assembled in their shop. One of their shop people had made a mistake in assembly. That was why they always had an instructor take a new glider's first flight, to catch just such mistakes. My glider would definitely be ready for me when I returned, mechanically perfect and test flown.

I was looking at my calendar to book another five days when Matt interrupted. Wasn't it right that I had no place to fly back in Kentucky? No hill with a landing zone at the bottom? Was I going to be able to fly only at Lookout Mountain? He was sure I realized what a highly skilled activity hang gliding was, how much practice it took to stay competent, to stay safe, not to mention improving. If I were only able to come back occasionally….

He was only articulating what I had been worrying about over the whole week. How was I going to be able to fly? It was the same problem as with sailplanes.

"You might not know," said Matt, "that we manufacture a motor carriage here at Lookout."

A motor carriage? What in the world was that?

As it happened, Matt had one down in the shop, newly completed for another customer. We went to look at it.

It was an ungainly little thing, like a tricycle-mounted lawn chair with a single-cylinder engine and propeller bolted to the back. It weighed a mere 95 pounds. Hung beneath an ordinary hang glider wing, Matt said, it created a self-launching micro-trike that could be flown from any old farmer's field, or off the pavement of an airport. Matt called it a sky cycle, and he showed me how the carriage folded up small enough for the back of a pickup truck…or the top of my Volvo station wagon. He had a two-place teaching trike—a much bigger and brawnier thing—in a hangar down at the LZ, and an instructor. If I wanted, I could book my next session at Lookout when the instructor and teaching trike were available, and see how I liked it.

I had another long phone conversation with Libby. I put down a deposit on a SkyCycle carriage.

If my first week at Lookout Mountain was one of the peak experiences of my adult life, my second week, a month later, was a decided anti-climax. It rained three of my five days, the resulting absence of any hill or tandem time made all the worse by the fact that I had elected to set up a tent on the LZ rather than sleep in the crowded bunkhouse. The only bright spot in the sodden days was the SkyCycle. The newly-completed carriage, all bright and shiny, had been brought down from the ridge-top shop to the "motor hangar" on the LZ. My wing had been repaired and laid out beside it. Ron helped me set it up, and when the assembled wing was raised and the craft stood before us in all its dragonfly splendor, I was excited indeed. It was just terminally cute. I strapped myself into the seat, put my feet onto the front wheel pegs, and pulled in the control bar. It felt real. I could definitely visualize myself flying in it. I was sure I had done the right thing in buying.

I never knew whether the instructor was sick that week or just mad at Matt, but he didn't show himself at the Flight Park on either of the two days of flyable weather. I had a SkyCycle I could assemble and disassemble, but nothing else to show for my five days. I had to go back to Kentucky.

Matt was ambivalent about my taking the SkyCycle. He absolutely didn't want me trying to teach myself to fly it, and he worried about the temptation. He knew too many wannabe hang glider pilots who had tried to teach themselves to fly and killed themselves in the process. The early history of ultralight aircraft was filled with similar stories. He didn't want me to be one of those guys. He would be getting another two-place instructor. I needed to come back anyway to get my hang gliding to where it needed to be for me to "solo"—run off the high ridge. On the other hand, he didn't want to store the carriage and wing. He didn't have secure room, and he couldn't guarantee they wouldn't be messed with. In the end, I signed a sort of contract (though I was sure it wasn't legally binding) saying that I wouldn't fly the SkyCycle until I had been signed off by a USUA-certified instructor. Ron and I loaded the SkyCycle—carriage and wing—on the top of my station wagon and I set out north for Kentucky. Every time I stopped people gathered to look at and ask about it.

Back in Kentucky, I searched the USUA magazine and the internet for trike instructors. Lucian Bartosik, out in the western part of the state near Hopkinsville, was the only full-time instructor anywhere around. Matt didn't know him, but Matt didn't have any ideas about a new instructor for his operation either.

I called Lucian Bartosik.

Now, three weeks later, I'm in Hopkinsville with my SkyCycle and hang glider. For six hours in five flights, I have sat in the back seat of Lucien's teaching trike, looking over Lucian's head in its white helmet. My feet, like Lucian's, are perched on pegs, though mine are just footrests. The lower pegs steer the nose wheel, for taxiing on the ground. The engine's throttle is a pedal atop the right peg. The brake pedal for the nose wheel is atop the left.

Lucian taxies us out from his hangar to the runway, takes off, achieves a comfortable altitude, and turns things over to me. At his orders I practice turning to specific compass headings left and right, at various degrees of bank. I practice these turns going fast, with the nose down, going slow, with the nose up. I practice stalls, straight ahead, left and right, hating the falling, floundering feeling at the top of the stall, but knowing I must react instinctively to regain control if I slow down too much.

All these maneuvers are accomplished by pushing and pulling on the bottom bar of the triangular control frame that hangs down between the front seat of the trike and the tiny windshield. Lucian in the front seat has only to raise his hands to chest level to grasp the bar. From my perch behind him I have to sit up and reach around, squeezing up against his back. He is generous about this, bobbing about to give me clear sight lines so I can turn accurately.

I thought a lot about Superman when I was young, and at some point with Lucian I have noticed that the bar control movements I use to fly the trike look a lot like the ones Superman uses when he flies. When I pull back on the control bar, we dive and speed up. When I push out the nose rises and we climb.

Pushing the bar right turns us left, and vice versa. I understand why all this happens, a matter of shifting our center of gravity, just as with hang gliders. But I did not notice it with hang gliders. Only when I was practicing these motions sitting in a motel chair with my arms extended, pushing out and pulling back, pushing left and right, tilting my body appropriately, did I think about Superman.

Aside from that connection to my youthful fantasies, though, I have been disappointed in my relations with the air in Lucian's trike. For the most part, Lucian and I have flown only in the early morning and late afternoon, when the air is cool and still. This was true of my hang glider flying too. But whereas the lightness of the hang glider and the delicacy of the control response made flying in even these conditions thrilling, "flying" the trike in calm air might better be described as "driving" it. With the throttle underfoot, one directs the trike and it performs as directed, like a car with three dimensions of control. There is no sense at all of wheeling and swooping. The few occasions when we have flown the trike in live air have not brought the senses of wheeling and swooping I fantasized either. Rather, my control motions have produced what felt like almost a continuous state of lurch—up and down, back and forth, falling off on one side, then the other. I had some of the same feeling in a sailplane and was sorely disappointed by it. My sailplane instructors flew with minute but constant motions of stick and rudder. I wondered how many hours of flying it would take me to master that unconscious control.

"Don't work so hard," Lucian says. "Your arms will just fall off on a long flight. Let the wing sort out the bumps by itself."

I try to relax, to soften my iron grip on the control bar, to let it swing mildly back and forth, left and right. Lucian narrates me along.

"Just left pressure here; release. Left pressure; release. Right pressure, hold; release. Nothing. Nothing. There. That's a strong thermal on the left wing tip. Right pressure, hold, hold, hold; and release."

Lucian came to the U.S. on the invitation of a British couple who were running an ultralight flying school in Colorado. A few years later he joined another partner in Hopkinsville. The U.S. Army's Fort Campbell was nearby, housing the 101st Airborne Division with its helicopters and aerial tankers. His Hopkinsville partner predicted that all those flyboys would be crazy for aerial recreation on weekends. A self-taught ski professional, hang glider and trike pilot fluent in German—like Lucian—should fit right in.

Back over the field, I have graduated to the front seat of the trike. Lucian sits behind me now, mostly silent. I am nervous every morning, but once strapped into the trike I settle down and take off confidently, pushing the bar out as I mash the throttle pedal to the stop, waiting briefly for the trike to hop off the ground, then pulling the bar back to accelerate in ground effect. We climb astonishingly quickly, the runway leaping away below us. At 1500 feet I throttle back to level flight.

We are working on navigation. Today we are going to the Jefferson Davis monument, some ten miles southeast of the field. Lucian has given me a compass heading to fly. I am to hold course and altitude until I see the monument. "Don't worry," Lucian has assured me. "You'll see it."

I had read that the monument marks the site of Jefferson Davis's birthplace. I had also read that, at 351 feet, it's the tallest unreinforced concrete structure in the world. I see it a long way off, a slender, silver-gray obelisk spearing above the trees. As we near it, I see men working on the sides, suspended on ropes.

"I always give them a show when I come over here," says Lucian. "Today it's your show."

I ask what I am supposed to do.

"Fly tight circles around the structure," says Lucian. "Show off the trike." I do, but my first two circles are not tight enough for Lucian. "Get closer in," he shouts over the headset. "Bank it right over." The men are hanging in their harnesses, three men, waving x-patterns with both their hands as I swoop in. I am closer than I am comfortable with. But not close enough for Lucian.

"I've got the trike," he shouts, and as I take my hands off the bar he cranks up the hand throttle in the rear and banks the trike over until it looks like we are standing on the down wingtip. The g-force from the turn presses me into the seat. I can see that one man is holding a sandwich, see the stubble on all their faces. Three tight circles we make, a helix down the side of the monument, the workmen whooping and gesturing. Then we're off, Lucian righting the trike at high speed, treetop level.

"Your airplane," he shouts, and I lurch forward to grasp the bar, my heart thudding. "Take us home."

Flying back to the field gives me time to calm down and then re-clench at the prospect of landing. The trike will take off mostly by itself, but landing is another matter. Which is a shame, since, as the old flying saw has it, "Taking off is optional; landing is mandatory."

To land the trike I have to get myself in position about 200 yards from the runway threshold and 200 feet in the air, cut the throttle, and glide down to within a wingspan of the ground, about 30 feet, after which I have to push the bar out to bleed off speed and set the trike down smoothly. It doesn't sound difficult, but for me it is. For one thing, I have to keep the trike aimed straight at the threshold throughout the descent. The little zephyrs that the wing dealt with by itself at altitude now I now have to be overcome with quick, precise responses. Close to the ground I have to push the bar out at just the right rate, not too fast or I'll stall ten feet off, not too slow or I'll be directing a rolling tricycle missile. Left, right, back and forth I jerk the bar. I think again about learning to ride a bicycle. This time, it's down a steep hill. Over an uneven surface. In a gusting cross wind.

I have been fighting with landings from the beginning with Lucian. It's frustrating, since I had no trouble landing a sailplane or a hang glider. But a sailplane has three axes of controls, and a hang glider can be "rolled in" on little wheels attached to ends of the control frame. There is something about the mass and speed of the trike and the limitations of control with the bar that buffaloes me.

Lucian's instruction is not much help. He learned all his skills—skiing, hang gliding, trike flying—without instruction, his feel-mastery developed by trial and error. He doesn't know what to tell me, or how to guide my motions with the bar, simply demonstrating over and over, landing effortlessly, perfect every time. But I'm too high, too low, too fast, too slow, off to the left or the right. I explore every combination of maladjustment. Six or seven landings in a row and I am exhausted, drenched in sweat, trembling. And Lucian's frustration has ratcheted up his voice and his temper:

"No, no, NO! You were horribly high on the flare. Couldn't you see that? Do you want to collapse the landing gear?" …

"I thought we were going straight into the hedge that time! The runway's three bloody wingspans wide. You don't have to scribe the mathematical center, but you should stay in the county." …

"The bloody gusts will come, you know. They absolutely will! You can't control the wind, so you have to respond to it."

At the ends of the last two days, Lucian has apologized. He understands that he "sort of" gets behind on his temper occasionally. But surely I can understand his frustration, when I'm doing everything else associated with flying the trike so well.

I wonder if he can understand *my* frustration. I know I'm in a bad rut, and something needs to be different, but I don't know what. This is so far from my fantasies about flying. And my time on this instructional expedition with Lucian is running out.

The goal of the week's flying is for me to solo. Lucian needs to have enough confidence in my flying ability to turn me loose in my trike. My Skycycle holds only one person, so solo is the only way to fly it. Lucian has flown it, and he's declared flying it to be "a piece of cake." He assures me that if I can fly his heavy and fast trike, I will have no trouble flying the lighter and slower SkyCycle. He will provide for me a USUA-sanctioned endorsement, fulfilling the terms of my purchase contract for the SkyCycle. Then I can take it back to central Kentucky and cultivate a deep acquaintance with it on my own. But I absolutely have to be able to land.

Alone in my room, I rehearse landings mentally over and over, while I'm showering, brushing my teeth, trying to get to sleep. But even these rehearsals are not successful. I always "black out," lose the thread of my visualization somewhere close to the ground, a symptom of what I do when I'm actually flying. In the deep night I wake up thrashing from muddled dreams—searching endlessly from the air for a landmark on the ground I can't find, trying to fly the trike into my home garage. Headaches accompany these awakenings. I take aspirins and try to go back to sleep, fighting my brain to keep the landing rehearsal fugue at bay.

The night before the last full day with Lucian is the worst I have had in years. I wake up sweating, brain whirling, an appalling pain occupying the whole left side of my head. I take three aspirins, try to lie down again; can't, from the pain. Is this just stress, or am I having a stroke? Should I call 911? I try to keep my breathing under control, check for other stroke symptoms: no drooping facial features as I squint in the bathroom mirror, no weaknesses in my arms or legs. I walk the floor. Literally. First time in my life. After a while the pain abates. I actually sleep a few hours before dawn, but I am a wreck. I think I should call off the day's flying, pack up and go back home without soloing.

Out at the field, though, Lucian is excited. No breath stirs the air, and the sky is full of pink popcorn clouds.

"It's a magnificent inversion," he says.

I know about inversions, know that normally the air gets colder as you go up in altitude, know the reason: the air close to the earth's surface is warmed by the sun's surface heating and cools as it rises. On rare occasions, say when a cloud layer forms over the earth at night and there is no wind, cool air may be trapped next to the surface, and only the air above the clouds gets heated by the early sun. That's the inversion. The cool air will just sit until enough sunlight gets through the clouds (ultraviolet radiation goes through clouds) to heat the surface and start the normal pattern. This breaks up the cloud layer, though it's still warm above them. That is what we are looking at.

Lucian can't wait to get up.

I don't say anything about the way I feel.

It's cool as we rise from the ground, cool enough that I wonder if I should have worn a long sleeved shirt. Too late now. We rise toward the cloud layer, the bottoms absolutely even. I ask Lucian what I should do.

"Climb above," he shouts.

I pick a clear space between clouds and rise through. The air is immediately warmer. From horizon to horizon the sky is filled with evenly spaced clouds, clouds the size of houses, with occasional small buildings, a few stadiums, all perfectly white. Below the clouds the air is clear, the earth green and brown checkerboard with clusters of houses and barns. Above us the sky is absolute blue. The edges of the clouds are very active, thinning and thickening as I glance about at them. It is a thrilling scene. I think how glad I am not to have missed this.

"See that little cloud over there," says Lucian, pointing to a cloud the size of a house, about 300 feet away. "Fly over to it and around it, coming out on the same heading we are flying just now."

The cloud is dead ahead and a little below us. I hold our course and pull in the control bar slightly, diving towards the fluff. Just in the short time it takes us to get there, the cloud has dissipated slightly, the edges wispy and diffuse. But it's still coherent enough to fly around, so I bank right to go out well beyond the edge. As I start my left turn Lucian says, "Get tighter up to the core. Get close but maintain your visibility. There. Now hold that precise bank angle and take us right around."

I hold the bank tighter than I had planned in the still, warm air, feeling the g-force and the slight sense of dizziness as we go around, the wisps of white fleeing past. About the time I know we must be nearly around the cloud I realize that I don't know exactly what heading we went in on. I was concentrating on the cloud. To set a heading, I should have picked two landmarks in a line, out well ahead on the ground, so I would know to level out when I got lined up with them again. I decide it's best to admit this rather than guess.

"We're almost around but I don't know exactly," I say into the spongy mike.

"Why not then?" rejoins Lucian, mildly.

"I didn't pick landmarks before I went into the turn."

"Well, that's not so good, is it," says Lucian, but still mildly. I wait for the edge to come into his voice, but it doesn't. He is enjoying this. "This is too good to worry about headings," he says. "Just fly around between the clouds. Have some fun."

This is the first time Lucian has given me permission to "have some fun," and I don't know what to do. "Do you want me to tell you where I'm going?" I ask.

"No," he says. "Just maintain your altitude and fly between the clouds."

So I do. The clouds fill about three-quarters of the sky, the spaces between them resembling passages and byways. I pick a passage to the left and turn towards it, turning harder as I get near the wispy edges, holding that turn between the clouds, now banking into a right turn to follow the edge of the right-side cloud. Out into a blue I see a cotton ball house dead ahead. I push the bar out and add a little power to rise gently over it, then pull the bar in, come off the power, then sink into a right turn and another passage, the wisps breathing by on both sides, perhaps ten yards to whiteness.

We emerge into a bigger clear area. I relax my grip and let the trike float through it as I look across to the other side for the best opening.

"This is so much fun!" I can't help but say this. Swooping and diving among porcelain clouds on a perfect fall morning in a tiny open airplane—it's completely visceral flying, so easy and effortless even I can almost forget the airplane is there at all. This is what I have yearned for, all the years since my teen models.

"These are amazing conditions," says Lucian. "In my two years here I've had only one other day like this."

The clouds are thinning out now as the earth's heating accelerates and the air warms. Ahead is blue sky to the horizon. Off to our left a half-mile is one of the last stadium-sized clouds.

"I want you to go and fly through the heart of that cloud over there," says Lucian, in a serious way.

This prospect disconcerts me. It's a pretty big cloud. Looking across my left shoulder at it, I see the whiteness going to grayness as I look into the center. "Isn't that illegal?" I hedge, never knowing when I'm being tested about something, maybe this time the FAA rules for flying near clouds.

"Yes," says Lucian cryptically. "But it's something I want you to experience and this is a perfect situation for it—no other clouds and I've done a clearing check for other aircraft. Turn left now. I want you to be dead level when you enter the cloud."

I push the bar out firmly to the right. The trike tilts over 30 degrees to the left and executes a strong turn. I push the bar left against the turn, the trike levels out, and we fly straight at the cloud, now 100 yards away. I can see its flat bottom a good deal below me. It towers above, in tufts and tendrils. By now I can't even see its edges, and its forward tendrils are reaching out to us.

"Straight and level," says Lucian, quite seriously. "Hold straight and level. We'll be out the other side in less than ten seconds, but it will seem longer."

I grip the bar hard. The forward edge of the cloud seems to rush out to envelope us. It is dappled white for a moment and I'm conscious of my attention going to my peripheral vision, where things are clearer. But now everything is completely white, growing quickly darker to a medium gray. The air is suddenly cooler and misty, but I am totally focused on seeing and there is nothing to see. The gray rushes past, no shapes at all in it, nothing but homogeneous gray. I have this immediate fear of running into something and I grip the bar harder. But there's no way to slow down, nothing to do but rush forward. Abruptly there's a warm patch and I am assaulted by a damp, fetid smell, like a clothes dryer with laundry left too long wet. My goggles mist over, which doesn't make any difference as there is still nothing to see. All at once it is a little lighter, then a lot lighter, then there are shapes of light and dark, then I can see out the white into the blue beyond. We sweep out of the cloud into the blue, the warm, the clear.

It is an incredible relief.

The trike is banked over about 20 degrees to the left in a moderate turn. I am gripping the control bar as hard as I can. I have been the whole time. How can we be in a turn?

"Are you going to level out or not?" barks Lucian.

I push the bar left to level out, then visibly slump as I relax.

"Didn't like that much, I would say," intones Lucian, again imperturbable. "That's good. You should never do that on purpose. As you saw, it's entirely disorienting."

I acknowledge that vehemently. He goes on to remind me of the fact that I went in straight and level, came out at a 20-degree bank, and hadn't a glimmer that I was doing so. He asks if I know why and I say I do. I know all about the failure of one's inner ear to detect constant bank angles when one loses the visual horizon. I know about John F. Kennedy Jr.'s spiral into the waters of Cape Cod with his wife and sister.

"That's good. I figured you'd know the theory and something about the history. Now you have a piece of the experience. That's very important, Roger. You know the theory. You know the rules. You have the experience. There's no excuse for getting into a cloud."

Theory and experience. I think as I fly us back to the field that they are finally coming together for me. I know I have to spend the rest of the morning on landings, but I'm not as clenched as I was coming back from the Jefferson Davis monument.

And my landings are better. Of ten, one is nearly perfect, but all the others are competent. Lucian relaxes and I do too. That helps my flying, I'm sure. I am filled with quiet satisfaction when we break at midday, actually looking forward to resuming in the late afternoon.

I am not disappointed. My afternoon landings are as good as the morning ones, better even. Four out of ten are nearly perfect. After the tenth landing Lucian directs me to taxi the trike back to the hangar. I clamber from the front seat, Lucian following. We remove our goggles and helmets. The sun is almost setting, the air cool.

"Well, Roger…ready to solo?" Lucian looks me in the eyes. "I say you are."

I am. I don't want to think about it—just do it. We fuel the trike. I pull my helmet on, climb in, goggle and belt.

"She'll fly lighter without my weight," Lucian says, loud, so I can hear despite the headphones. "She'll come off quicker, be more responsive. You know that. Just do what you have been doing. You'll be fine. Three touch-and-goes." I plug in my headphones, realize there's no point to it. I won't be talking to anybody. Lucian gives me a thumbs-up. I taxi out to the taxiway very carefully, turn right onto the runway, taxi out to the end, turn the trike around. I have an impulse to look back at the hangar, but I don't. I take a deep breath, push the control bar out, mash the throttle pedal to the stop.

Lucian is there to meet me as I approach the hangar. I have been watching him ever since I turned off the runway, standing in front of the great sliding door, his arms fully extended over his head, waving. I am filled with a warm feeling for the whole human condition.

I also see that Lucian has pulled my SkyCycle trike out of the hangar. It perches jaunty behind him, red-white-and-blue wing tilted over. It's surely too late to fly it this evening, but I will if Lucian wants me to. I can do anything.

"Looks like we have a new trike pilot," 'Lucian shouts as soon as my helmet is off. He is beaming at me. We shake hands and slap backs. I feel wonderful.

That night I take Lucian out for a steak dinner. We talk a long time. We also talk about tomorrow. I need to leave tomorrow, to be back home by dinnertime. Lucian's plan is for me to solo the SkyCycle first thing in the morning—fly three touch-and-goes, then play around some if I want. After that we'll break it down, put it on the top of my Volvo. He has some ideas about how to secure it better than I have been. Then I'll be off, off to home, off with the skills to fly the Skycycle on my own. An instructional week well spent, coming together in a good way at the end.

I go to bed happy, really happy, and sleep soundly the whole night.

When I look out the window of the EconoLodge at 6:30 a.m. I can't even see across the parking lot. The world is packed in fog. At 7:30, after my Complimentary Continental Breakfast, I call Lucian.

"No problem," he says. Fall morning fogs burn off with at least an hour of great flying before the sun heats everything up.

At 8:30 it's still foggy and I call him back.

"Let's go on out to the airport," he says. We can talk about securing the folded up Skycycle, and be ready when the fog breaks up.

By 10 a.m. the fog is breaking up. More precisely, it's being blown away. A sticky little wind has picked up. With the wind the fog leaves fast, but the sun is hot and the air steamy, not much like the cool stillness of yesterday afternoon. As I fill up my fuel tank, I start to clench.

Lucian is unconcerned. He walks around the SkyCycle, performing a last check on wire connections.

"Ready to go?" he asks brightly, then, maybe with a look at my expression, "In an hour you'll be on your way home; nothing but fond recollections." I think a little sourly that that wouldn't be the case anyway, but I'm feeling generous after yesterday. I hope he's right.

I climb into the narrow sling seat of the Skycycle, fasten the belts over my shoulders and waist. I pull on a different helmet, one Lucian has given me without built-in headphones. It doesn't fit as well as the one I have been using all week, but I decide to say nothing about it. Lucian steps back, gestures above his head to the wind sock, counseling a last look. I follow his gesture with my eyes. I already know the wind is coming from about 45-degrees left of straight down the runway, a partial cross-wind. I don't like it, but I can't back out. I get a sudden flash of my first run off the big hill at Lookout Mountain, a worse misery of tension, instructors and other students all standing around, watching. I couldn't back out then either, and it was fine. I hope it will be fine now.

I reach up and pull the starter cord attached to the mast above my head. The engine coughs into life, and I can feel the propeller whirling behind me. I will warm up the engine taxiing out to the runway threshold. I undo the Velcro strap that fastens the control bar to the mast, needing a quick grab to control the wing as the wind jerks it.

I look one last time at Lucian. He stands impassive, a half-smile, holding a thumbs-up. I return the gesture, press the throttle. The SkyCycle rolls forward.

The trike leaves the ground quicker than I expect, and I can tell as soon as I'm in the air that the flight will be much different from yesterday's smooth circuits.

The SkyCycle is like a cork in moderate surf, bobbing and bouncing. I fight the control bar; no time for gentle grips here. Above the tree line the air is a little smoother, but I still feel very light and very vulnerable. I think of just flying around a bit, hoping for familiarization, but I'm too uncomfortable, too anxious. The air, I know, is only going to get more boisterous as it heats. I want to be back on the ground, to do my three touch-and-goes as quickly as I can and stop flying.

Two hundred feet up on my first approach and I am fighting the bar more than ever. I pull in to add speed and the bar pulls back at me strongly, but when I release tension the trike bobs up 20 feet. I am too high, and have no confidence I will be able to get the trike on the ground in the length of the runway. I press the throttle to go around.

I exhale as I climb, trying to settle down despite the trike's bouncing. I tell myself that I can do this. I did it yesterday: 20 landings. 20! No. 23. Surely I can do three today. I find myself wishing I had the heavier trike.

I go around on the next pass too. Fifty feet off the ground a gust of the cross wind blows me so far off the right side of the runway that I am not sure I can recover and re-center myself. As I throttle up and climb again, I glance at the wind sock. The wind is stronger. I have to get down. Landing is mandatory. I have to land now. It's only getting worse. A fleeting image of the sort Lucian used in his critiques of my flying flits across my consciousness: the trike landing half sideways, half-off the runway, the wind catching the wing, the whole trike with me in it cartwheeling.

I push the image away.

I am grim on the third approach. I will get down. I have the bar pulled in as far as I can hold it, the trike approaching its top speed. I am going to just drive down through the turbulence, not countering it, just powering through. My mouth is tight across my teeth. My arm muscles are trembling.

At the end the ground comes up too fast for me and I hit, hard, my helmet knocking against the mast. But I am down. I concentrate on keeping the wing under control and the trike rolling straight, slowing, conscious of my heart pounding. As I turn up the taxiway, I see Lucian running toward me. He is shouting.

"What in the bloody hell did you do? You never flared a bloody degree, that's what, just drove it straight into the ground. All that practice, and you just drove it in. I have it on video. You never pushed out at all, just straight in. I have no idea what you were thinking."

He would have gone on, but I was driving past him.

"Where the hell are you going?" he says. "Did you break something?"

Back at the hangar, out of the trike and my helmet, I try to explain, telling him the turbulence is more than I can handle in the light trike.

"That's bullshit," Lucian shouts. He insists I can handle it. One bad landing doesn't mean a thing. I have to get right back up on the horse. If I want, he will fly a circuit, show me how straightforward landing the SkyCycle is.

I resist the urge to shout myself. I begin disassembling.

"What the hell are you doing?" Lucian is off again. He can't endorse me for the SkyCyle with a single landing, and a bad one to boot. I have to stay another day. Or come back. Surely I understand that.

I understand that I am not staying. I can't. I have other commitments. As for coming back…I don't address that. I don't know myself what I think about it.

When Lucian sees I am determined to go, he settles down and helps me. We load the carriage and the rolled and bagged wing on top of the Volvo, tying them in a new pattern Lucian has devised. It is more secure. I thank him for it. I can tell he doesn't want me to leave like this, without closure, the ends of the intense week dangling. He offers to take me to lunch. But I am adamant. I have to get on the road. Part of me, the confrontation-averse part, wants to apologize. But I'm not sure what I would apologize for, and I know this situation—whatever it is—is not all my fault. I will pick it to pieces in retrospect, but I don't want to now.

I stand formally, hold out my hand. Lucian shakes it, cocks his head a little.

"We'll get together again," he says. "I know it. You'll do the right thing."

I nod, climb into the Volvo. I wave as I bump out the access road of Lucian's field.

I wasn't going back. By the time I got home to central Kentucky, I knew that. I knew enough, had enough touch, to teach myself. I knew there was a local farmer whose property had once been an active private airport. He still maintained, mostly for old time's sake, a landing strip, a wide grass expanse. I would make my best appeal to him. If he would let me fly from his strip, I would have the luxury of waiting for perfect local air.

Then I would have all the time in the world.

Belonging

I am standing in front of what looks to me like a great expanse of white corrugated aluminum, 14 feet high and 40 feet wide. It's the front of a hangar. Inside the hangar resides an airplane. But I am not thinking about the airplane. I am thinking about Arthur, a hang glider pilot I met briefly at Lookout Mountain, five years ago.

Arthur lives in what looks like an ordinary residential house a mile south of the operations building at the Lookout Mountain Flight Park, down the road on the narrow ridge top. The house is one story, with gray cedar shakes. It has white window trim all around, and a white porch across the left half of the front. A white double garage door balances the right side.

You wouldn't know the garage sports an identical door at the back.

Arthur took an early retirement buy-out from a computer consulting firm in Atlanta. He and his wife Shirley moved to the Lookout Mountain ridge specifically so he could hang glide as much as possible. Shirley works in Chattanooga.

Out the small deck along the back side of the house is nothing but sky. The Sequatchie Valley lies spread out nearly 2000 feet below, the view tapestried with small farms, squares of green dotted with whites of houses and browns of barns. Across the wide valley other lines of ridges stretch to the horizon.

Most days in the spring and summer, Arthur gets up about 6 a.m. and slides through the screen door out onto the deck. Shirley remains asleep in their bed. Peach-colored light bathes the hillside. Wisps of fog float in the folds. Back in the bedroom Arthur pulls on shorts and sandals, pauses in the kitchen, on the way to the garage, for a glass of orange juice.

Inside are two sensible Toyota Camrys. In front of them, fully assembled and pointing to the back of the house, crouches a hang glider, lime green and white. Arthur pushes a wall button and the rear double door of the garage pivots up, letting in the peach light, the sky, and the Sequatchie Valley. Stepping into the triangular control frame of the glider, Arthur lifts it onto his shoulders, and shuffles out onto the extended concrete pad behind the garage. He returns for his harness and helmet, straps on, hooks in, stands up, takes a deep breath and runs right off his dewy back yard into the sky.

It takes him about 20 minutes to float in undulating s-es to a soft farmer's field below, the land wheeling in slow motion beneath him, the air sighing in his ears. The grass tickles the sides of his feet as he skims in. The farmer likes the novelty of hang glider landings in his side lot. Arthur has wooed him with honey-smoked hams and good conversation. Looking far up the ridge, Arthur sees his house on top, a gap in the trees.

I am thinking about Arthur this morning as I stand before this hangar. Behind me is an acre of asphalt, edged on one long side by a seven-foot-tall chain link fence. I'm feeling isolated, out beyond the fence, at the edge of this lake of asphalt, in front of this great aluminum wall.

At waist level in front of me is a padlock. I turn a key, twist a connector, hear and feel some large fixture moving on the other side. I push in. A tall seam opens from top to bottom and a ten-foot-wide section accordions in. I push and pull other accordion seams until the whole front of the hangar is open.

Inside is the airplane. It stares straight out at me—the Cyclops eye of the curved, green-tinted windshield, the beaky blue nose of the prop spinner with its nostrils of cowl cooling ports, the straight black mustache of the propeller above the square mouth of the air filter.

I own this airplane, a two-place 1969 Cessna 150. For me, owning it is like owning a lion. Interactions with a lion are largely on the lion's terms. So it is for me with this airplane, and at this early stage of ownership and interaction I have only the roughest idea what the terms are. I do know if I mishandle the airplane on the ground, repairs will involve parts mailed in from far away and the work of a certified aircraft mechanic, expensive and inconvenient. If I mishandle the airplane in the air, orderly flying will be interrupted, scaring me, maybe even killing me. Airplane ownership is a serious business.

In order to learn what the airplane does and does not permit I have retained the services of the flight instructor at my local airport. Michael Day is in his mid-20s, fresh-faced and blond, with a football player's build. His newly-minted business card designates him as CFI-I/C/SEL/MEL. This means he is a Certified Flight Instructor, certified by the Federal Aviation Administration. He is an Instrument-rated instructor, meaning he can fly without looking out the windows, and teach others to do so. He is a Commercial-rated pilot, qualified to fly for hire, in Single-Engine and Multi-Engine, Land-based aircraft. He went to a lot of trouble, a lot of training and expense, to obtain all these certifications and ratings. He is working as a flight instructor at our local airport to accumulate enough hours in the air to apply for jobs as a commercial pilot. He is paying his dues.

I am going to fly this airplane today, with Mike Day in the right seat beside me. In order to prepare to do so, I get out my Pre-Flight checklist. It is flip-page two of a packet of checklists, a collection of laminated pages spiral-bound across the top. The Pre-Flight checklist is very detailed, telling me cryptically just what to do in what order to insure that my airplane is ready to be flown.

All the checklists in the packet are similarly detailed. There are lists for preparing the cockpit prior to starting the engine, for starting the engine, for preparing to taxi into the hubbub of airport operations. There are lists for taking off and landing under normal conditions, for cross-wind-conditions, for fields that are soft and/or short. There are lists for dealing with the engine's stopping on the takeoff roll, stopping just after takeoff, stopping in flight, a list for an engine fire on the ground or in the air. Reading through the checklists is unnerving.

Each checklist component abbreviates a world of background, of faults and consequences. Take the "engine oil" component of the Preflight checklist that I am currently working through. The oil dipstick is accessible through a little door on the passenger side of the engine cowl, secured with two wing-nut latches. I twist the wing nuts and swing the little door up. Inside, just in front of the battery, is the round, yellow top of the oil dip stick. I unscrew this top and draw out the dip stick, leaving the tip in the snout of the filler tube. I wipe my finger down over the oil that has climbed up the stick while the engine has been at rest, re-insert the stick, draw it out again, and scan the dark oil line. It's half-way between the "4" and "5" marks, about right. Oil capacity for the engine is six quarts, but if I fill it up with six quarts, oil will spray out the breather tube when the engine runs at high rpms, which it must do a lot. The sprayed oil will be messy to clean up. On the other hand, the manual for the airplane says not to run the engine with fewer than four quarts. Doing so will cause excessive friction. The engine may heat up, might ultimately seize and be ruined. What I have discovered is that about the four-and-a-half-quart indication keeps any oil from spraying out, and is suitable for flights of two hours or so. If I were to go on a longer flight, I would fill to five quarts and carry a quart with me.

Thirty minutes of checklist checking finds me ready to pull the airplane out of the hangar. To do this I use a tow bar. The tow bar reminds me of a stethoscope. The ear ends of the tow bar fit over little knobs on either side of the airplane's front wheel, with a t-handle where the ends come together. I attach the ear ends to the knobs, kick aside the chocks that keep the front wheel from rolling, grab the t-handle, lean backwards, and pull. The airplane rolls grudgingly and I pull more, walking backwards, slightly turning the front wheel as I do so. The airplane turns in front of me, and I finish my crab walk 20 feet out in front of the hangar, turned sideways to it. The Manual cautions to start the pull-out straight. Turning the nose wheel when it is stationary may stress the linkage, as may swiveling it more than 30 degrees when it is rolling. The airplane is sideways to the hangar to keep the prop blast from blowing everything inside around when the engine starts. I open the pilot-side door under the strut and reach behind the seat into my flight bag to get my headset. I unwrap the double cord from around the ear pieces, free the microphone arm on its swivel mount, and plug the two ends—one for the radio, the other for the cabin intercom—into their differently-sized receptacles under the dash board. We—the airplane and I—are ready to go, as far as I'm concerned.

I look up to see Mike Day sauntering towards me across the ramp.

Mike Day shares none of my sense of strangeness and portentousness about airports and my airplane. An acre of asphalt is to him a somewhat smallish space in which to park and maneuver airplanes. My hangar with its 14-by-40-foot façade is about as small as a hangar can be. My Cessna 150 is lead-pipe simple, a basic, two-place trainer. It is as docile and non-threatening as a good bicycle.

Mike does his own "walk-around" of the airplane. He doesn't use a checklist. This is because he knows exactly what to look for. His eye flies over every linkage, every level, every angle of the airframe. He knows what everything is supposed to look like, so anything that does not look right will just jump out at him.

This is part of the difference between Mike Day and me. But there's more to it than that. I'm worried about missing something in the preflight inspection because what I miss might intrude on the orderly progression of my flight. Then I'll be in big trouble. I won't be able to compensate for it in the cockpit. Mike has an immensely greater repertoire of cockpit skills. He's pretty sure he can handle anything.

Owning an airplane for Mike would be more like owning a car than owning a lion. A car is not entirely predictable. It may break down occasionally, and you probably can't fix it on the spot. But the situation is not likely to terrify you, or kill you. You never think about it like that. For my airplane, I do think about it like that.

So today I will go flying with Mike Day, trying to emulate his calm confidence and the knowledgeable precision of his airplane handling. He will tell me what sort of take-off to do—normal, short field, soft field. We will rise up from the airport and at 500 feet turn west, out over the rolling countryside of central Kentucky, where people to be disturbed by our droning maneuvers are few and fields to practice setting up emergency landings are plentiful. We will practice slow flight, stalls, 360° (exactly) circles at a 45° (exactly) angle of bank. We will practice circling at a fixed distance around a point on the ground, practice flying half-circles back and forth across a straight road. We will climb, descend, turn to specific headings. And when I take a long breath, beginning to wonder when the lesson will be over, Mike will invariably say, "Where is the airport?"

I will peer out the windows, looking for landmarks. About all I know for sure is to go back east, toward the interstate highway. Mike knows exactly where the airport is, to the nearest degree of the compass and nautical mile out. I don't know how he knows. He's oriented in the sky like an experienced hiker is oriented in the woods.

Back over the airport, I will go through the Pre-Landing Checklist and set up my approach. I will fly the rectangular landing pattern and try to stare the runway threshold into compliance with where I want it to be when the airplane is ready to touch down. I will flare too late, or too early, too high or too low, too fast or too slow, off-line or off-center. But not too terribly too ever, and the airplane, docile trainer that it is, will get itself onto the ground and roll straight ahead. I will take a deep breath, flip the toggle switch to raise the flaps 20 degrees, push in the knob that controls warm air to the carburetor. Then I will advance the throttle, glance at the engine gauges to be sure they are in normal ranges as the engine winds up to full rpms, focus down the runway, and take off to go around again.

Today—as on many other days—I have to remind myself why I am doing this, why I am seeking entrance to the world of General Aviation. This flying shares almost nothing with the lovely intimacy of hang gliding—the naturalness of the control bar, the soft tickle of standup landings in the grass. It shares hardly more with the SkyCycle, repository of my hopes for an approximation of what Arthur has with his and Shirley's house on the Lookout Mountain ridge. Why then am I now hanging around hangars on acres of asphalt, apprenticing myself and my checkbook to an all-up certificated metal aircraft, assaulting my fantasies with checklists for engine fires aloft? Why am I subjecting myself to unnatural flight attitudes at unscannable altitudes, reducing the landscape to compass headings and nautical miles?

Shortly after I returned from western Kentucky and Lucian, I presented myself at Miller Lackey's farm, ten miles north of my house in Berea. In 1939 Miller's uncle, Sam, graded 2400 feet down the family farm's east side and created an airstrip. By the 1950s it was an active community airport, with a flux of colorful characters, a tobacco-barn hangar, and 25 light airplanes tied down along the taxiway leading from the 1857 farmhouse. Locals called it Lackey International Cow Pasture. By the time I arrived, there were but four forlorn airplanes in the dingy hangar, with two more tied down in tall grass along the taxiway. All the other planes had left, for one reason or another, and only two of the planes remaining were flown regularly. Still, Miller, at age 82, kept the runway green and smooth, and local pilots circulated by to chat with him about the good old days.

Miller was skeptical when I showed up with the SkyCycle on top of my Volvo. I put it together beside the Lackey family farmhouse while he looked on. He'd never seen an airplane like it before, he said, never seen one where you could move the wing around. He walked all around it asking questions, questions about the structure, about weight, fuel capacity, engine performance, takeoff and landing distances, climb, glide. When we adjourned back to the kitchen of the house, he grilled me about my training credentials. I outlined my experience at Lookout Mountain and with Lucian without giving too many details. "Well, hell," he concluded at last. "Light as that thing is, if you crash it you're not gonna kill anybody but yourself." He gave me permission to fly the SkyCycle from the strip and keep it in the barn, though I had to remove and fold up the wing each time I flew and cover it and the carriage with tarps. There was no door on the barn. "I don't want anybody coming in here to look at that thing who shouldn't be on the property," Miller said.

For the next two summers, dead-calm late afternoons found me faithfully at Lackey International. It took me 45 minutes to set up the wing and attach it to the carriage, strap on the five-gallon gas tank, pull on my helmet, my flying jacket, and gloves. Belted in, I'd pull the rope starter twice, the engine would bounce into a crackling roar, and I would grab the control bar and taxi out.

The trike leapt off the ground in the first 100 feet of the runway. It climbed at 500 feet per minute. I flew at 1500 feet, cruising over Berea, where athletic teams would stop their practices to look up at me as I passed over. When I flew along Interstate 75 next to town, I could see cars pulling off the road to watch me. Occasionally one would dash off an exit and follow me back to Miller's farm, the driver full of questions after I landed.

There were a few issues. One day after I had cycled through ten take-offs and landings, a neighbor appeared at the end of the runway. Her husband worked nights, she said. He needed to sleep during the day and the racket from my two-stroke engine was keeping him awake. I promised not to repeat the exercise.

I was also not soaring. The dead-air flying was certainly enjoyable, almost as good as Arthur's morning sled rides down to the floor of the Sequatchie Valley, but it was not my yearned-for engine-off bobbing and weaving among the mid-day thermals. One day in the second summer at Lackey's, I did gird my courage to try a mid-morning flight. I took off and bounced up to 1500 feet, but when I considered shutting off the engine, I quailed. I was bobbing and weaving all right, and much more in control than I had been in my first flight with the SkyCycle at Lucian's, but it was still more than I was comfortable with. After a half hour I had enough and powered down, only to get blown about by thermal turbulence so badly on my landing approach that I landed hard and broke my wing's keel.

Back at Lookout Mountain Flight Park for repairs, I was told by the new trike instructor that the SkyCycle was really a "dual eight" flying machine, best flown before eight a.m. and after eight p.m. I really hadn't understood that before then.

I didn't have much time to think about the implications for my flying, however, because Miller Lackey died of a cerebral aneurysm that fall. He had cut the runway earlier in the day, was drinking iced tea on the back porch of the farmhouse. He just keeled over. Not a bad way to go. But with Miller gone everything else went too—120 acres, the barn, and the 150 year-old farmhouse. His widow and sons asked the earth for the property. They got it, too—from developers.

There was another grass air strip in my area, but it was an hour's drive away. Loading my wing and SkyCycle on my Volvo, setting up and taking down, would have multiplied this time considerably. I would have had to guess about good air, guess hours in advance.

Just four miles from my driveway, the county airport stretched its long asphalt arms, but I had had little to do with it since my discouraging conversation about sailplanes five years before. I did go out to talk to the airport manager about flying the SkyCycle there, and while he couldn't refuse me use of the airport, he was not at all welcoming. I put the Skycycle in my garage and didn't fly at all the year after Miller died.

One day I got a call from the county airport, not from the manager but from a pilot friend who knew of my flying frustrations. Would I by any chance be interested in a Cessna 150? A very nice one was about to be put up for sale, neatly installed in a private hangar on the airport grounds. I could take over the whole arrangement, learn to fly "a real airplane," he said, at my beck and call 15 minutes from my door.

I had a serious conversation with my wife. I bought into General Aviation.

I have to say that learning to fly the Cessna—learning to fly in the Cessna—was a lot of work, with periods of considerable stress. A private pilot's certificate granted by the FAA permits an individual to fly a properly-equipped airplane into any airspace in the country. That's a huge privilege, and the FAA does not grant it lightly. The FAA medical examiner who certified every two years that I was physically fit to fly asserts that the training for his pilot's certificate was the second-most intellectually and physically demanding training of his life, just after med school. I agree with the spirit of his comparison.

About halfway through my training, my instructor, Mike Day, left to take a job with a regional airline. It was just what he was hoping for, but it left me with the necessity of finding another instructor. The instructor I found was an old hand, and there was a transitional period in which I had to learn his way of thinking in the airplane. But after that we were able to work well together. I studied for and passed the FAA knowledge test, and in the difficult weather of a winter and spring I soloed, flew my cross-country, night, and instrument requirements, and passed my practical test. It was hard and it was stressful, suffused as I was with the feeling that I was grappling with environmental and mechanical worlds that were bigger and more complex than I could cope with. But I met the FAA's requirements. I was a certified pilot, owner of a capable airplane I could fly whenever and wherever it was safe to do so.

The first thing I did was to try to find a way to get back into soaring.

The first strategy I tried was to join Kentucky's only glider club. It was in Bardstown, renowned for Stephen Foster's "My Old Kentucky Home" (though Foster never lived in the South) and several high-class distilleries. Bardstown was almost halfway across the state, but I hoped that substituting a 50-minute Cessna flight for the two-hour drive to the field—besides being just plain fun—would make all the difference. Unfortunately it didn't. Flying the Cessna across the state was fun all right, but adding the time required at my county airport on both ends of the flight, the difficulty of gauging summer weather, the necessity of scheduling with a club instructor, and the one-hour limit on club glider flights, I saw after two years that club training was going to be as unworkable as it had seemed before the Cessna.

There was, of course, the Chilhowee Gliderport, four hours south of my home, where earlier in my quest to be in the air, Gil and I had flown for a couple of days. In the five years since our time there, it had experienced a renaissance. A young Canadian woman with a basket of flying credentials and boundless enthusiasm had acquired the operation, put it on a secure logistical and financial footing, and turned it into a real soaring mecca. Sarah Kelly (now Sarah Arnold) told me over the telephone that in three to five days I could accomplish all the training and testing required for my glider add-on certificate. No caveats.

Sarah was right. In five blustery March days (though none with a wind rotor over the field), I flew my dual and solo flights and passed my second practical test. I was a certified glider pilot, having finally—if circuitously—gotten to where I wanted to be after my first experience at Bermuda High six years before.

But I still had no way to soar conveniently.

I did try soaring the Cessna occasionally. When I felt a thermal boost during a flight I would throttle back and lower the flaps a notch or two. The Cessna would fly level at 60 miles per hour under those terms, but it wouldn't climb. Any climbing would be the result of rising air. But climb it did. On hot summer days I could routinely circle up 2000 or 3000 feet, right up to the base of the clouds. Once I soared some 20 miles without touching the throttle, ending up 1500 feet higher than when I started.

The problem was the engine. It didn't like running that slowly for extended periods. I had to clean spark plugs repeatedly, and my mechanic told me I was in danger of burning exhaust valves. It just wasn't the kind of flying the Cessna was designed for. But the kind of flying the Cessna was designed for was not the kind of flying I yearned for. One symptom: fuel costs were about $20 an hour. I could afford that, but the engine's sucking 100-octane leaded aviation fuel to run constantly out in front of me did take the purely joyful edge off just going for a couple of hours of sightseeing.

The fact was, I wanted deeply to be able to soar on a regular basis. But even with all the time and effort I had expended, the two main ways to do that—bring a sailplane to me, or bring myself to where there were sailplanes—still hung out there, unreachable as ever.

While I wondered, I tried simulation. Flight simulators have been around ever since WWII, when the venerable Link Trainer provided military pilots the opportunity to experience something like flying without external visibility. More recently, vastly complex (and correspondingly expensive) full-motion simulators have become an essential component of advanced and recursive flight training, particularly for airline pilots. But desktop simulators—most notably Microsoft Flight Simulator—have brought aspects of the flying experience across a wide range of aircraft to everyday desktop computers. While the Microsoft program does feature a glider, the simulator soaring pilots talked about in *Soaring* magazine was called Condor.

Condor was developed by two Slovenian software engineer/glider pilots specifically as a soaring competition simulator, where pilots in pure sailplanes could compete on-line for fastest flying around a stipulated course…in Slovenia! Initially, the physical geography of the program was entirely Slovenian, but in the years since Condor's introduction (and in the years since, the second iteration, Condor2), independent designers had provided geographies from all over the world, as well as some fictional ones. I bought a copy of Condor and spent many hours with it, no doubt improving some of my flying and airborne strategic skills. But "flying" with a fourteen-inch laptop screen, a mouse, and a set of rudder pedals was far from ideal.

During the winter after I added my glider rating, Libby and I spoke seriously about the bringing-me-to-where-there-were-sailplanes option. Maybe I should try going to an exciting place where I could saturate myself with soaring for a short time in a rental sailplane. Maybe periodic ventures of that sort would be enough. I made reservations for the following summer for five days at a premier, motor-glider-based commercial operation in Arizona.

I hadn't figured on forest fires. My five days of flying were suffused with smoke and fire-fueled turbulence. My instructor and I were not able to do any cross-country flying. Though I learned a lot, and enlarged my experience with a new breed of glider, it was really not satisfactory. There are so many variables in a successful soaring experience. Having them all optimized during a brief visit that had to be planned months in advance was a low-probability event.

By late summer of 2013 I had more or less decided to take the flying the Cessna gave me, which—I had to admit—would once have been beyond my dreams. By then my plane was comfortable and familiar. For days after a long Cessna flight my fantasies would be full of it, as I changed the scenario in little, always positive, ways, filled with a warm excitement. The Cessna and the airport world it was embedded in—both physical and social—had become good friends. In my best moods I thought I could live with that. Besides, I was approaching my 70th birthday, and I had read that insurance companies were reluctant to write insurance for post-70 pilots.

For the world of soaring beyond the Cessna, I would just read *Soaring* magazine, enjoy simulated soaring in Slovenia with Condor, and continue to enjoy my fantasies. After all, I had been doing elements of that for nearly 60 years.

Silent

Two months later, an airplane for sale jolted me out of my resolve. It was an Alisport Silent 2 Targa. It was Italian, all fiberglass and curvaceous carbon-fiber construction. A self-launching sailplane, it possessed a retractable engine, making it joyously independent of tow planes.

The Silent appeared initially in an on-line aircraft classified ad publication.

Not many sailplanes appeared in the publication. But I had long admired this premier component of Alisport SRL's product line and I had never seen a used one for sale. This Silent was not only for sale, it was being listed by a pilot who lived in Knoxville, just two hours away, a pilot I actually knew of, though I had never met him, and knew nothing of his ownership of such a sailplane. I could even afford something in the neighborhood of his asking price.

I showed Libby the ad. "If I don't at least go look at this," I said, "then I am truly, irrevocably, writing off ever owning a sailplane."

"Let's go look," she said.

There's no suspense in the final outcome. I bought the glider. There's no suspense in the events of the ensuing two years either. Maintenance issues associated with the engine kept the glider grounded for almost all of that time. But there's value in the story, and in all the learning that preceded the perfect flight I recounted at the beginning. Here's the story.

Three days after my conversation with Libby, we met Joachim Schneibel at the Downtown Island Home Airport in Knoxville. Schneibel is a German, a retired physicist in the Oak Ridge National Laboratory's Metals and Ceramics Division. He is a long-time sailplane pilot, an ex-instructor in sailplanes and motorgliders. Out at the Island Home Airport we drove in Joachim's car through the secure ramp gate onto the ramp. Off by itself crouched a gleaming white sailplane trailer. The three of us climbed out of the car and stood looking at the long, long trailer. Joachim said something, but I wasn't listening. He fumbled in his pants pocket, emerged with keys, bent over, unlocked and unlatched the top of the trailer, stood aside, and motioned for me to lift it. I grasped the handles and tugged up, finding the lift heavier than I expected, grateful for the gas struts that supported the trailer top. Inside, nestled compactly on dollies and racks, were all the components of a glorious sailplane.

I have to say I had a strong dreamlike sense, a sense of unreality. Here was for me an absolute fantasy situation—exactly the right sailplane in what appeared to be immaculate condition, right here in front of me. I realized I was actually considering buying it, had vaulted into that state as soon as the trailer was opened.

"Drop the trailer tailgate," Joachim said, all business. "We'll roll it out and put it together."

The next two hours would be an intense blur for me were it not for the detailed photographs Libby took. I have them in a file on the hard drive of my computer. They chronicle the rolling out of the fuselage, the rolling out and attachment of the right wing, then the left, then the elevator, Joachim bending, kneeling, sitting, stretching, a series of choreographed moves whose subtlety I would not appreciate until I tried to duplicate them on my own. In half an hour there was the complete glider. I look at a photograph of Joachim and me side by side, arms folded identically, just staring at it. I remember being nearly overwhelmed.

When Libby and I got home I called the North American distributor for Alisport. Leonardo Benetti-Longhini is an aerospace engineer within the aerospace complex housed at the airport in Tullahoma, Tennessee. Leo knew this particular Silent well, having arranged for its import seven years previously, having picked it up at the port of entry in Maryland, trailered it to the first owner in Arizona and checked it out there. Joachim had consulted intimately with him in purchasing the glider and bringing it to Tennessee. Leo verified everything Joachim told me. The glider was in essentially as-new condition.

Next I called the insurance company that works with the Soaring Society of America. A friendly account executive there said they would write insurance for me and the glider, subject to two conditions. I would need a log book sign-off from an instructor attesting to my competence in flying this type of sailplane—one with a retractable engine. And I would need a signed-off cockpit check-out from someone familiar with the particular glider. That would be Leo.

Within a week I had made Joachim an offer. I would buy the glider and trailer, but I didn't want to take delivery until the following spring. I wanted him to look after the glider over the winter and maintain his insurance, up until the FAA-mandated annual Condition Inspection in April. If the Condition Inspection didn't reveal any unexpected difficulties, I would pay him then and take possession. Joachim agreed, even offering to repair some hail damage to the trailer over the winter. I set about finding an instructor with a retractable-engined self-launching sailplane.

There weren't many in the U.S., only four on the list published by the Auxiliary Powered Sailplane Association. I wrote to two. One was no longer instructing, but the second was and was reasonably nearby: Steve Dee in Memphis, an ex-Air Force pilot who flew for Federal Express. He had an almost new two-place Slovenian sailplane. Steve Dee and I made a date for September.

Two weeks before the date he emailed to say that the sailplane had been caught in a hangar fire. The insurance company had declared it a total loss. He had a new one on order from Slovenia. It would take six months to be delivered.

All winter I waited, with periodic updates from Joachim about progress on the trailer repair.

The trailer was finally finished that April, just in time for the glider's annual Condition Inspection. Joachim had established a relationship with an aviation mechanic who worked on sailplanes. Tim Grater had an extremely broad knowledge of exotic sailplanes. The only trouble was that he worked only at his house in the Knoxville suburbs, having experienced some friction with the powers-that-be at the airport where Joachim kept the Silent. Because the glider had its own trailer, this didn't present any problems. Nor did my flying buddy object—Joe Sanchez, also a mechanic—who agreed to come along with me for the inspection. After much juggling of schedules we all congregated at Tim's house on a sunny Saturday morning in mid-April.

Joachim had pulled the glider in its trailer over from the airport. We all ate sandwiches and assembled the sailplane in the grass of a side yard. It was a convivial occasion, with Tim's explaining his inspection checklist as he went along, Joe hovering over Tim, Joachim telling stories of his own maintenance activities. I stood back, taking it all in. In a way I—as The Buyer—was the most important person there, yet I was so clearly the least knowledgeable and experienced that I felt like the odd man out.

The inspection, at least, was entirely satisfactory, and I got to run the engine for the first time. But I couldn't take possession of the glider. My insurance coverage was contingent on my having the self-launching sign-off, and Steve Dee still didn't have his new sailplane. Finally, in May, it was delivered, and I made arrangements to journey to Memphis for my instruction.

Shall I say that the weather was suspect until the last minute? That a frontal passage gave us only two good—if turbulent—days to fly? That Steve Dee's Slovenian glider—with retractable landing gear, constant-speed propeller, and sequential flap deployment on take-offs and landings—was far more complicated to fly than anything I had flown before? Shall I admit that on the last flight, when we attempted some real soaring, I got airsick from the constant tight-circles I was trying to fly? It was not my finest hour. Still, Steve Dee signed my logbook. I could take possession of my glider.

But I couldn't fly it. I needed the cockpit checkout for that.

On a Friday in early June of 2014, I journeyed to Knoxville with Joe to complete the sale with Joachim and drive on to Tullahoma. I had seen the glider assembled and disassembled only twice, once when I first visited the previous September, and the second at the Condition Inspection, so Joachim and I had scheduled another session for me to go through the assembly and disassembly processes myself. But thunderstorms in the area threatened to descend on us, exposed as we would be out on the ramp, so we agreed simply to execute the FAA paperwork to transfer ownership.

I handed Joachim the largest certified check I had ever dealt with, and he handed me a box containing every piece of paperwork ever generated by him or the previous owner in the course of their ownership of the glider. Sale and registry documents were signed and witnessed, and we proceeded out to the parking lot where Joachim had pulled the trailer. Raising the top, he pointed out three boxes of spare parts, a serious tool box, a complete set of all-weather covers for the glider, and a parachute. A parachute was not required by the FAA or the insurance company, but this one came with the glider, custom designed as "a very expensive seat cushion" as Joachim explained. I had known about all of this gear, but hadn't appreciated what it amounted to until then—certainly as complete a package as one could ever hope for. I didn't have much time for appreciation, though. With the sky darkening, we hurriedly hooked the trailer up to my van. It looked about a block long. I had pulled boat trailers, but never anything remotely as long as the glider trailer.

Joe and I eased out of the parking lot at the Island Home Airport about 4:30 p.m., looking hard at the dark western horizon. It was right on the front edge of Knoxville's rush hour. Within 20 minutes we were crawling along in traffic on the interstate highway in the middle of a vicious thunderstorm, with me glancing every few seconds in the rearview mirrors at the sailplane trailer stretching out behind. What an introduction to sailplane ownership!

Saturday with Leo Benetti in Tullahoma was a long day. We met at the giant Tullahoma Regional Airport (a WWII bomber training base) at 9 a.m., removed and assembled the glider (no trouble with an experienced rigger overseeing the operation), extracted the engine, and for the next six hours (with no lunch), Leo went over every system and construction detail of the engine and airframe. His knowledge was encyclopedic. If I had been able to absorb it all,

I would have been able to pass a test on the factory construction manual. As it was, Joe did make a very good list of things to look out for, pre-and-post flight, seasonally, annually.

About 5 p.m., Leo had me don the parachute—my first time ever in a parachute—then helped me over the side of the Silent into the cockpit, strapped me in, explained all the controls, and sent me off on a round of taxiing on the vast ramp, getting used to the large radius turns necessary with the long wings and tiny steerable tail wheel. I returned, we talked, and he sent me out again. We did this for about an hour, until I had demonstrated that I could turn to predictable headings in both directions and fast taxi at least for a short distance with the tail up and the wings level. Leo cleared me to fly. A few cumulus clouds still frothed above us. "Go on up to 3000 feet or so," Leo said. "If you find a thermal, soar around a bit. Have fun. I'll endorse your log book while you fly."

My gosh. I should have been thrilled at that moment. This was, after all, the realization of a 50-year dream. I was about to take a high-performance, self-launching sailplane that I owned up for the first time. I was about to have fun in it. It should have been one of the peak moments of my life. But I was tired, sunburned, dehydrated. I probably shouldn't have been flying at all. But that was what I had come for, and Joe and I had to leave the next day.

The glider taxied straight, took off, and climbed much better than I expected. I climbed through 3000 feet, hesitant to shut off the engine. At 4000 feet I finally did, going carefully through the cool-down, prop-centering, engine retracting steps. I didn't raise the main wheel, but even with it down, the airplane was a joy to fly—straightforward, simple, responsive. I was just on the verge of having fun when Leo called on the radio. I looked so good that he wanted to come up and fly too and take photos. If I would come down while he got his electric-powered version of the Silent out and assembled, we could fly together. I thought about declining his offer, but I felt obligated. So I spiraled down—giving away all of my 3000 feet—and landed, a little harder than I would have liked, but competently.

My second take-off was not as good as the first. As I approached flying speed I found the glider inexplicably pulling to the right. I pushed in the left pedal, pushed more, but still veered. I was just about to pull the throttle back to abort the flight—facing an excursion off the runway into the grass and a possible bad outcome—when I realized I had flying speed. I pulled the stick back and the glider lifted off, over the grass. No harm done, and I doubted Joe and Leo had even noticed. But it had been a bad moment for me.

It was fun flying with Leo. I got to see what the glider looked like—what I looked like— in the air, and that was pretty thrilling. The cumulus clouds had dissipated though, and the air was settling. I set the glider up for landing and flew the landing pattern, approaching the runway at the right speed and what I considered the right attitude—dead level, rather than the nose-up attitude I was used to in my Cessna. I was surprised when the glider banged down hard again. Maybe I did need to pull the nose up a little, a little more "flare" as pilots say. I would have liked to do some more landings to understand the proper attitude, but it was late, and there was no time for another cycle. Leo had landed and started his electric motor to taxi back to his trailer. I extracted my engine and did the same. The engine sounded a little louder than I remembered, but I was too tired to pay attention.

I was too tired to help with the disassembly either. Leo pronounced my flying "better than average for a first time" as he and Joe took the glider apart and stowed the pieces in the trailer. Only one detail marred the moment. The prop-centering procedure depended on a tongue-depressor-shaped rubber blade that the pilot extended after the engine was shut off. The propeller was rotated with the starter to stop vertically against the blade and stayed that way as the engine was retracted. The pilot was then supposed to retract the blade by means of a little lever in the cockpit. I had forgotten to do that when I shut the engine down the last time in the air. When I restarted the engine to taxi, the prop hit the blade on every revolution. That's what made it sound louder than I remembered, and normally that would have been no problem. The blade was made of rubber precisely to anticipate such forgetfulness. But that time, the vibration in the blade had broken the connector cable. Leo said he had never seen such a thing before. But there it was. The engine couldn't be run again—and for me the glider would be unflyable—until the cable was replaced.

In spite of this, I was a very happy camper that night. Joe and I ate at a Mexican restaurant, and I started with a 22-ounce mug of beer to restore my electrolyte balance. I owned an absolutely wonderful glider. All the conditions of my insurance had been met. I had flown it. I had fun with it. I was surely looking forward to the summer.

It didn't work out quite as I hoped.

Back at my airport in Kentucky, I discovered in Joachim's collection of spare parts a replacement prop-stop cable. But the resident mechanic at the airport was busy with Cessnas and Pipers and not eager to dive into such an odd bird as an Italian self-launching sailplane. Joe agreed to journey over to the airport to do the work, but he was not available for a while.

I used the rest of June figuring out where on the airport grass to park the sailplane trailer—there wasn't room on the ramp—and how to assemble and disassemble the sailplane that it was designed to carry. There were subtleties in the process I had not appreciated in the two times before when I had seen it done. I learned about these subtleties in fits and starts, clumsily, frustratingly, sometimes agonizingly, as in failing to execute a sequence properly and finding myself holding one end of a long wing that needed manipulating at the other end, or feeling the fuselage twisting in my hands after I failed to tighten a hold-down strap. Watching me try to manipulate the pieces of the glider became entertainment for airport denizens. At least I didn't break anything.

Summers are busy times for Libby and me, and I didn't get back to the glider until August. Joe came and replaced the prop-stop cable, and I began to learn to navigate under power along the ramp, taxiways, and runway of my airport, all much narrower and occasionally more crowded with other aircraft than the giant Tullahoma airport. I moved my Cessna out of its hangar onto the ramp and left the sailplane assembled inside, squeezing my hips carefully around the six-inch clearance on either side of the wings, and that without the removable wing tips.

At the end of that first summer with the glider—the end of all the fraught assembling and disassembling, the slow taxiing on ramp and taxiways, the fast-taxiing on the runway—I flew the glider exactly twice. The first time was encouragingly uneventful, up and down in the last glow of a fall afternoon. The second flight was not so encouraging.

I flew when the air still had a little bounce to it. I was eager to see what the glider could do in lively air, so a little late-afternoon bounce—about what I had flown in at Tullahoma—seemed an appropriate stepping-stone. I climbed to 3000 feet, turned off the engine, and went through the procedure to center the propeller, levering the prop stop out and tapping the starter to move the prop a few degrees at a time. I had had no difficulties with this on my previous three flights, but now I did. The propeller came around to being nearly centered, but then flipped past the prop stop. It did it on the first revolution, then the second, the third, the fourth. All this time the glider was losing altitude, with the stilled engine providing a bucketload of drag. I was just beginning to entertain thoughts of landing with the engine out—and vulnerable to shocks—when, on the fifth try, I finally got the prop to stop centered, not perfectly, but enough for the engine to retract. I was greatly relieved. I was also about out of altitude. Bouncy air forgotten, I set up my landing.

I was happy with the landing until the last moment, when the glider bounced off the asphalt. It wasn't a bad bounce, but it put the glider in the air again, slow and veering off to the left. I pushed the nose down and stepped hard on the right rudder pedal. The glider stuck when it touched down again but continued veering to the left. I hauled back on the dive brake lever, which clamped the brake, but the left wingtip went off the runway and down into the edge grass, cutting a long arcing swath before banging back onto the asphalt. The glider came to a stop pointed about a 30-degree angle right of the centerline. I sat, waiting for my heartbeat to return to normal, desperately glad the wing had not contacted a runway light. Finally I was composed enough to extract and start the engine…and shut it down immediately. I had heard the now-for-me telltale noise of the propeller striking the prop stop. Distracted in the air by the difficulty in centering the prop, I hadn't retracted the stop blade after the engine folded away. Distracted on the ground by the landing, I had not retracted it before I started the engine. The propeller had only hit the blade a few times, but my post-flight inspection revealed that the stop at the end of the control cable—a little hollow cylinder with a hole in it and a set screw to tighten against the cable—had loosened and been flung away.

I called Joe, the mechanic. He said he was sure he could find an equivalent replacement, but it would take him a while. It was November.

That was the end of my 2015 flying season.

My home airport manager thought he would be able to find winter storage room for the trailer in our airport's group hangar, but by December it was clear he couldn't. I absolutely did not want the sailplane and trailer outside for the whole winter. Forty miles south of Berea is the London-Corbin Airport. There I found a hangar to rent. Angled just so, the trailer barely fit into the hangar, inches at the back and front.

That's where the sailplane spent the winter.

Over that first sailplane winter, I noticed that I had lost my soaring fantasies. The first symptom was my loss of interest in *Soaring* magazine. For almost five decades, I had read the magazine from cover to cover the day it arrived, then gone back and read many of the articles a second and third time until the next copy arrived. But November's issue sat unread on a table in our family room, to be joined by December's. Looking at the covers gave me an inchoate negative feeling, a little queasy, a little stressed.

I also ceased imaginatively to jump skyward when interesting clouds gathered overhead. I still noticed clouds, but any effort to visualize myself up among them was accompanied by the same negative queasy feeling, the same sense of stress. I found myself turning my gaze down, away from the sky.

It was in my sleep-time rituals that I finally acknowledged what was going on. Where for most of my life I had been able reliably to transport myself into an imagined soaring scene to still my inner daytime dialogue and lead myself to sleep, any such attempt now led me instead to one of the difficult scenes of my recent actual past experience. Whereas before I could visualize myself pulling up in car-and-trailer alongside a runway in an exotic soaring location, and a moment later being towed up into a blossoming sky, now I was assailed with recollected images of my mishandled sailplane assemblings. My previous fantasies of effortless releases from tow or simple switch-off engine shutdowns were overridden by the realities of my prop-centering episode. Long final glide fantasies of sunsets and whisper-true landings were swamped by the memory of my uncontrolled bounce and off-runway wingtip excursion.

I understood that much of the problem was caused by the rarity of my actual experience: maybe ten assemblies, only four flights. If I had landed a hundred times, say, one or two difficult ones wouldn't have troubled me. But I wasn't going to get a hundred landings anytime soon.

I put aside soaring fantasies altogether.

I went to the London airport over the winter a few times to charge the glider batteries and check on things, but I didn't open the trailer until the Condition Inspection. On the April day appointed for that, Joe and I pulled the trailer down to Knoxville and set up—in Tim Grater's side yard as we had the previous year. Joachim met us. I still didn't have a cable stop for the prop stop, so that was the first difficulty we faced.

The second was that the tail wheel tire was flat. Closer examination with the fairing removed revealed that the tire was sliced, presumably by some metal or glass it had encountered on the asphalt of my county airport. The hub was abraded and cracked. I had never given the tailwheel assembly more than a cursory inspection during pre-flight checks. Probably I had been taxiing on the flat tire enough to crack the hub. Maybe that had been the trouble in my last landing, with the uncontrollable left veer.

Everything else about the glider—except the prop stop cable stop—was fine, though. The engine started immediately, and though it seemed to have a slightly different sound from what I remembered and to vibrate a little more, Tim, the experienced mechanic, pronounced it fine.

Back at the London Airport, the manager offered me rental of a much larger and newer hangar at a good price. I jumped at the chance. Both the assembled sailplane and the trailer would fit into this hangar. Far better for me to spend 45 minutes each way driving to London than 90 minutes assembling and disassembling the sailplane every time I flew in Berea. Far better also than leaving the Cessna out on the ramp. The runway, taxiways and ramp at the London airport were all wider than in Berea. It was a good situation.

Over the next several weeks, Leo Benetti provided me with a new tailwheel hub and mounted tire. Joe found a serviceable cable stop for the prop stop. We installed both. It was early June. As far as I knew, the sailplane was ready to fly.

Libby accompanied me down to the London airport for the first flight of the season. We pulled the sailplane out, and I did a thorough pre-flight inspection, then together we pushed the sailplane 100 yards from the hangar to the edge of the ramp. I removed the wing and tail dollies, strapped on the parachute and climbed into the cockpit. Libby gave me a kiss just before I lowered and locked the canopy. I went through my cockpit check list (including checking the prop stop), turned on the master switch, extracted the engine, turned on the fuel pump and pushed the starter button.

The engine cranked around, but it did not start. This was the first time that had ever happened to me or, as far as I knew, to Joachim. I cycled the fuel pump switch to reset the engine control computer, and tried again. No start. No firing even. Two more times. The engine was dead—no sign of life. I had a dreadful feeling that another element was being added to a long sequence of discouraging situations.

Back at the hangar, I checked the spark plug head. It was completely dry, no wet residue of fuel. I tried shorting the plug out against the cylinder top. No spark. There was some kind of failure in the computer control of the fuel and ignition systems. How it could have developed since the Condition Inspection I had no idea.

I called Tim Grater in Knoxville. It wasn't too hard to convince him that it would be easier for him to come up to London for a diagnosis than for me to stuff the glider in the trailer and drive it to his house in Knoxville. He couldn't come for three weeks, though.

When he did come, he found engine pathology in about 15 minutes. After peering with his flashlight and mirror around and under the engine, he showed me a difficult-to-see crack in a plate connecting the engine to the mounting pylon. The crack ran under an electrical sensor, a sensor that kept track of the position of the cylinder. One of the sensor's connectors had been broken off. It was likely the sensor was kaput. Tim's hypothesis was that the crack had been developing for some time, but finally broke all the way through during the engine run-up associated with the last Condition Inspection. (We didn't discuss why the crack hadn't been discovered before.) An attempted restart of the engine at the Condition Inspection would have failed. But we didn't try a restart then, and I was left to discover the failure three weeks later. Tim took photos to send to Leo. Leo wrote back saying that parts would have to be ordered. From Alisport. In Italy.

Leo has a busy life, Alisport has a busy factory, and Libby and I have busy summers. All this added up to my not being home and in possession of the replacement parts until mid-August 2015. I got in touch with Tim again. Leo had estimated to him that the repair would take "two long sessions." I learned only as the repair progressed that Leo had never worked through it hands-on himself.

The first session established that a special puller would be needed to remove the flywheel, which had to come off to remove the broken attachment plate. Tim checked local auto parts stores. All rented specialty pullers, but none would fit the metric, Italian-crafted flywheel. Another call was placed to Leo. After a couple of weeks, Leo supplied a factory puller, but it proved too small, a reflection of the fact that design details for such a hand-fabricated aircraft changed over time. A puller obtained from an owner of a similar sailplane proved too flexible. Finally, a puller custom-fabricated by Tim did the job, the flywheel came off, and parts replacement proceeded.

Three work sessions had ensued already, Tim up to London from Knoxville, me down from Berea. Others were in the offing. The mounting plate supplied by the factory was not exactly the same as the one on the glider. Some drill press work (in Knoxville) was required. Some of the new fasteners were not the same diameters and lengths as those removed.

Through all this I got to know Tim quite well, acquiring a deep respect for his working principles. He was extraordinarily serious, patient, and careful, seemingly having imbibed the "First, do no harm" dictum associated with the Hippocratic Oath. He took nothing for granted, wanting to know exactly how things were supposed to come apart or go together before he turned a wrench or screwdriver on them. He measured, pre-fit, and checked everything. I am convinced this saved us on a couple of occasions from getting in trouble by forcing things. But this approach coupled with the vagaries of the factory-supplied parts guaranteed that the work would proceed piecemeal. When something wasn't as it was supposed to be, Tim called Leo for canonical advice on how to proceed. That introduced turnaround time, both because Leo was very busy, and because sometimes he did not have canonical knowledge. Tim journeyed from Knoxville up to London three more times before we were ready to run the engine again.

It was a cold, wet day, October of 2015 now, two whole years after I had bought the Silent. The last nut had been torqued and painted, the electrical components re-attached, and fresh fuel supplied for the tank. Tim and I would run the engine only a short time, he said, just enough so that any inadequately-secured components would reveal themselves. He and I walked through a kind of checklist for arranging the glider. We would turn it at the mouth of the hangar so the prop wash would stay outside, even though that meant the rear empennage would stick out into the rain. I would kneel beside the cockpit to proceed through the starting regimen and operate the throttle. Tim would brace the nose to keep the glider from moving forward further into the hangar.

"Remember that you can't take a moving propeller too seriously," he said.

We assumed our positions. I was conscious of the sound of the raindrops pelting the elevator at the back of the fuselage.

"Ready?" I said.

"Ready," Tim returned, crouching lower for better leverage. I went through the starting regimen, same as I had with Libby in June: master switch on, fuel pump on, starter button pushed.

The starter ground, the prop revolved, but there was no burst of energy from the engine. There was not even a pop. We tried again, but we both knew it was pointless. Tim stood up. I didn't, because I had noticed a light flashing on the instrument console, a red light. It was the warning light for low fuel, designed to come on as a solid warning light when fuel in the tank was low. It shouldn't have even been on. We had just supplied half a tank of fresh gasoline. It certainly shouldn't have been blinking. I had never seen it blink before.

"I'll tell you what I think is happening," Tim said. The computer that ran the engine was failing to get some vital signal and was announcing that with the blinking light. Either one of the electrical components the factory had supplied was defective or inappropriate, or something was not hooked up correctly. One way or the other, we were not getting electricity to the spark plug. Tim poked and prodded at the engine for another half-hour, while the rain beat down on the rear of the glider. I stood aside. I was pretty sure at that moment that I would not fly the glider that fall. I had not flown it over the whole previous year.

Leo would have to be called yet again, though I couldn't think what he could add to what he had told us already.

Tim took a few more photos. He would be thinking about the glider, he said. Maybe something would occur to him. It was, after all, a machine. If all the parts were assembled properly, it would work. The engine had run before. It would again.

We swiveled the glider back under the shelter of the hangar, the tail dripping. Tim got in his car and gave me a farewell toot as he pulled out into the gloom, sort of a "Be of Good Cheer" farewell, I thought. I pulled out clean cloths and dried the rear of the glider carefully, poking dry cloth into what few openings there were. The surfaces gleamed more-than-white in the fluorescent lights of the hangar. I stood back. The glider was a beautiful piece of sculpture, no doubt about that.

But right then, that's all it was.

The Off-Season

I stored the glider under immaculate conditions over the winter. The beautiful hangar at London was absolutely dry, but the glider had come with a complete set of all-weather covers and I had never even unrolled them. Now I did, marveling at the collection of fabrics designed for various purposes—water-proofing, sun-proofing, bug-proofing, ventilation—and all the vents, zippers, ties, and Velcro fasteners designed to mold the cover precisely to the glider's contours. I arranged the battery charger so all I had to do was plug it into the wall-receptacle. According to the charger manufacturer, I could have simply left it plugged in, its having been designed to sense an ambient charge and supply current appropriately. But I hesitated to just leave it. Besides, tending the batteries gave me an excuse to run down to London and open the hangar every so often on nice winter days. I would bring a magazine or a book, plug the charger in, and sit in a folding chair and read while the batteries were charging, just looking over at the glider occasionally to admire it.

When the weather began to improve in late March, I contacted Tim again. He had some new trouble-shooting ideas, he said. But in any case the glider was due its annual Condition Inspection. Even though it hadn't flown at all in the last year, it still needed a current Condition Inspection to be legal. Tim would come up to London to take care of it.

On the appointed meeting day in April 2016, I arrived early at the airport and removed and stowed the covers. They made compact packages, rolling up elegantly into integral pouches. The glider was almost dust-free, but I damp-wiped it anyway, marveling anew at the shiny, svelte contours.

The Condition Inspection proceeded duly with no revelations until it was time to run the engine. A simple check of the spark plug indicated that nothing had changed in that department since the fall—no spark at all. Tim had brought a sophisticated volt-ohm meter and set about clamping wires and measuring. I hung back, discouraged. It was clear Tim had no brilliant new ideas. He was just being methodical. I certainly had no plan B.

So I didn't pay much attention when Tim announced a few minutes later that the only thing he hadn't "got into" was a particular plug. He hadn't got into it because it was not designed to be gotten into. The plug was a junction, connecting little wires from sensors on the engine to the computer that managed the ignition system. It was sealed at the factory. To examine the connections of the wires, the plug would have to be cut open. Tim gave me a look.

"Sure," I said.

Tim extracted a Swiss Army knife from his pants pocket.

I was piddling around in another corner of the hangar when Tim shouted, "Aha!!"

"What?!" I shouted back, hurrying over to him.

"There it is!" he said. At my uncomprehending look, he continued, "The thing that's causing all this trouble. There it is, right there!" He produced a little LED flashlight from another pocket, shined it on the sliced-open plug lying in his hand. Four wires ran into the plug, four out, each outgoing wire soldered with a miniscule dot of solder to one incoming. But one pair had become disconnected. The incoming lead had slipped out of the solder joint. "That's the break in the circuit!" Tim said. "I'm sure of it."

I felt a kind of excitement welling up in me, for the first time in over a year. Could this really be the problem, something as basic as a solder joint, something not requiring any new parts from Italy? Tim turned to me. "I don't suppose you have a micro soldering pen?"

Part of my excitement drained away. Of course I didn't have a micro soldering pen. I hadn't ever even heard of a micro soldering pen. Tim didn't have one either, not with him anyway. We stood there for a moment. I was envisioning closing up the hangar yet again, Tim going back to Knoxville to return at some future date with the highly specialized tool. Then it occurred to me that there was another mechanic on the field, the resident mechanic. He was not resident very often, but I knew he had a full shop of tools. Maybe he...

"Oh sure," Tim said. "He'll have one. They're used all the time in working with avionics."

Well, as it happened the resident mechanic was indeed working that day, and he did have a portable micro soldering pen, which he would be happy to lend to Tim. For that matter, he would be happy to walk back with us to my hangar to see the glider. He had heard about the single-bladed propeller on the retractable engine, and he wanted to see it for himself.

The micro soldering pen was surely a cute tool, with a tip like a needle, heated by means of a drop-in butane cartridge. One simply lit the butane, waited a moment for the tip to get hot, and was ready to solder very tiny joints. Tim set about re-soldering the wires in the plug, while I walked around the glider with the other mechanic. We were both finished at the same time.

"You may be here at a historic moment," Tim said to the other mechanic. "We've been looking for this ignition problem for over a year."

I knelt beside the cockpit, rocked on the master switch, toggled on the fuel pump (noting, but ignoring the blinking red light), and pressed the starter. The click of the spark jumping from the sparkplug to the cylinder head was audible even where I knelt. I felt excitement growing in me again.

"Looks like you're good to go," said the resident mechanic.

"I sure hope so," I said, as he walked away.

I stood on one foot then the other while Tim married the two halves of the plug, taped it securely shut, zip-tied the cable where it belonged on the pylon, torqued in the spark plug, and pronounced himself ready to start the engine. We repeated our drill of the rainy day the previous October—the tail of the glider out of the hangar, Tim stationed at the nose, me kneeling by the open cockpit, reaching in. Master switch on, fuel pump on and whining away—a breath from me—starter button pushed. The starter clacked the propeller around half a turn—and the engine exploded into action! Tim and I exchanged huge smiles. He pumped his hand palm down, advising me to maintain idle, then after a moment raised it. I pushed the throttle, watched the rpms come up, followed his hand with more throttle as he leaned into the nose. Finally he sliced his palm across his throat and I cut the engine.

I was really happy in that moment.

"I'll look the engine over," he said. "But I'm pretty sure it's fine. Back to normal, at least."

"Back to normal." That was a wonderful place to be.

That spring of 2016, Libby and I were now seriously ready for our "summer of discovery" conversation: our determination to take a hard-eyed look at whether we were prepared to dedicate the time and resources to make flying the Silent safe and fulfilling for me. There were certainly concrete negatives in ownership—the 40-minute drive down to London from our house, the $250-a-month hangar rent, $2000 a year insurance. But more important was my attitude toward the glider. I still was far from comfortable with it. I put this down to the fact that I simply hadn't flown it enough. The few times I had flown it had all been stressful in one way or another, so that just thinking of flying it made me anxious. Lib pointed out that I had had a similar response early on in flying the Cessna. But after many flights and a store of pleasant experiences, I now approached flying the Cessna with almost pure positive anticipation. Would the same thing happen with the glider? This was what I wanted to find out. I determined to start with a careful and systematic program of ground handling.

I had depended mostly on my Cessna skills for ground handling the Silent on my first four widely-spaced flights. Now, with a 5700-foot-long, 150-foot wide, lightly-used runway at my disposal, I was going to get really good at Silent ground handling before I went airborne. After all, with the long wings of the glider only 30 inches off the ground, accurate ground handling was absolutely crucial.

I began by taxiing the glider from one end of the long runway to the other, back and forth. Operating by myself, I always had to start with the glider tilted over, one wing down on the asphalt (the upwind wing, if there was any wind). My first job, as soon as the speed came up enough to make the ailerons functional, was to raise that down wing. This was a precise left-right stick maneuver. If I pulled the down-wing up too fast or too hard, the glider would roll over to the other side, putting the other wingtip on the asphalt. During my early excursions I had real trouble preventing the glider from rolling, and since the drag of a wingtip on the ground (even with little skateboard wheels under the tips) slewed the glider to that side, I would be working the rudder pedals madly. It can't have been a pretty movie, the beautiful glider wallowing down the runway like a drunken seagull, rocking and slewing.

But I got better. As I added throttle, the glider went faster quicker and the tail came up sooner. The angle of the fuselage on the runway had to be controlled with back-and-forth movements of the stick, adding complexity to the left-and-right movements required to keep the wings level, but the rudder pedals in the faster-moving glider operated the rudder itself, which provided much more directional control than did the little tail wheel.

Landing presented its own challenges. The glider had to be landed horizontally on its main wheel, with the wingtips again level. As on takeoffs, the stick and rudder pedals would be in continuous motion, back-and-forth, left-and-right. As the glider coasted on its main wheel and slowed, its tail would have to be lowered delicately onto the little rear wheel.

One day during this process Tim called from Knoxville. When he hadn't heard from me he figured no news was good news, but in fact he had some news himself. Leo had tracked down the blinking of the low-fuel red light on the instrument console. It was doing just what it was supposed to do, announcing a half-full fuel tank: no light for the tank full-to-half down, blinking light for half-to-a-quarter, solid red from a quarter to empty. So that mystery was solved.

There were no mysteries left.

By Saturday, July 23, I was ready to fly. So was the glider. The engine had performed flawlessly for all the ground work.

There was nothing between me and the sky.

That first flight of that day was the first truly comfortable flight I ever had in the Silent. I have to say that it was one of the peak experiences of my life. As I taxied down the ramp toward Libby after the flight, I felt that I occupied a place of almost mystical union of sky and airplane. I could go soaring any time I wanted now, follow the sky anywhere it took me. It was a superb feeling of competence and endless possibility.

"I am so happy for you," Libby had said. "You've sure earned it."

I felt that I had.

Crash

After that first perfect flight in the Silent I considered not flying again that day. The first flight could not have been more thrilling. Why not take the memory home? But I knew intellectually I should go again. I needed to reinforce what I had just done, to add an increment toward second-natureness for the basic take-off and landing sequence.

So I raised my first finger skyward. Libby knew just what I meant. She stepped back.

I lowered the canopy and rotated the latches on the left and right sides into the locked position. I extracted the engine and went through the start-up checklist, making sure the prop stop was retracted before I pushed the starter button. I looked around for traffic, advanced the throttle, and began taxing back toward the runway.

I had just begun to roll when I noticed that the canopy was not properly latched on the right side. The canopy was secured by three latches—one each left and right by my knees, and a third, a pivoting latch at the nose that stayed attached all the time. Well, except at a Condition Inspection, when it was released to check that it would if a dramatic need arose, say if one had to bail out of the broken glider. The canopy was very light and flexible, so its edge sat in a groove that ran around the top of the cockpit wall. Sometimes when the canopy was lowered it would mis-mate with the groove near one of my shoulders, and when it did one of the back latch pins would not properly engage into its secure position. That's what was wrong in this case. I stopped the rolling glider, disengaged the pin, moved the rear six inches of the canopy a hair into its groove on the right side, and re-engaged the latch.

No problem.

I taxied to the edge of the ramp, turned onto a taxiway, drove along it to the runway head, taxied out onto the runway center. I made a radio call to announce my intentions. Then I reached for the throttle, rotating it to full on, and began my takeoff roll.

My roll was perfect this time, wings level and straight as an arrow. The glider rose into the air and started climbing. I climbed straight ahead until I was 500 feet up, then turned around—180 degrees—to come back over the runway. I was over the ramp at about 700 feet when I heard above the engine noise a little "thock" from around my right shoulder. Had I hit something in the air? A small bird, maybe? A large beetle? I peered out the right side of the canopy, craning my head to try to see the leading edge of the wing. It was only when I began looking around inside the cockpit that I saw that the right canopy latch had disengaged again. The canopy had risen about half an inch at the back.

I had no sudden reaction. I would just press the canopy back into place and hold it down while rotating the latch again as I had done before to re-engage it. It would be a two-handed operation, but I was pretty sure nothing much would happen when I moved my right hand off the stick. I did think I should land to see what was going on with the latch, and I was annoyed that my perfect second flight was going to be spoiled. But I wasn't really worried. I reached with my right hand for the canopy lip.

I was just beginning to press it down when the whole right side of the canopy lifted up.

It didn't lift much, just an inch or so, but it was clear that air had gotten under the canopy's whippy frame and moved the edge out of its groove. I had no way of re-seating it. The situation had instantly gotten more serious. I'm sure my heart speeded up, and two scenarios flashed into my mind, bolts of thought-lightning.

One was just to let the canopy go and land as quickly as possible. I didn't know what would happen if I just let go. Maybe the canopy would separate from the fuselage, fly off and drift to—and smash against—the ground. Replacing it would be expensive—communication with Italy, shipping and all—and would surely end flying for that year. Another year. This whole scenario blossomed essentially instantaneously in my mind.

The other scenario was to hold the canopy down as best I could, jerking my right hand back and forth from the stick to the canopy edge. I tried this out in instantaneous thought. Could I really preserve the canopy? Could I land the glider with only my left hand and intermittent jabs with my right?

My mind began adding questions. What if I let go and the canopy didn't just fly off? What if it twisted and flapped, still connected to the fuselage? Should I release the nose latch? What if the detached canopy blew into the propeller?

The propeller!

While my mind raced, the engine was running, the propeller whizzing behind my head. I reached for the fuel shut-off switch and the engine died, the glider nosing over. I jerked my hand back to the stick, brought the nose up, then back to the canopy. The engine was stopped, but still erected. What if the departing canopy slammed into the engine? What if it got past the engine but slammed into the elevator? Could I lose control of the glider entirely?

I was still in decision-making mode when the left back latch on the canopy let go. The canopy was now floating on both sides, and I needed both hands to keep it down. The glider sailed on, beautifully stable, and I spared an instant of gratitude for that. But it had now glided past the end of the runway, past the edge of the airfield even, and was losing altitude. I needed to make a 180-degree turn fast.

I skidded into the turn, relying mostly on my feet on the rudder pedals, with jabs at the stick with my right hand. The canopy was buffeting the whole time, and when the glider was half-way through the turn the front latch—only to be released in an emergency—unlatched by itself.

Now the canopy was truly free-floating, connected to the airplane only by my two hands. And though I was able to complete the turn, it was clear to me that the glider was not going to make it back to the runway, not with the drag from the canopy and the erected engine.

I was going to crash.

A kind of fierce calm came over me. I was going to crash. No help for it. A version of a remark from legendary aviator Bob Hoover bobbed up in my mind: if you're going to crash, fly the airplane into the crash. I determined to do the best I could to fly the glider into the crash. I just would. My focus was solely on crashing well.

I scanned briefly below me, saw two industrial facilities and a mobile-home sales park.

There was no chance of putting the glider down on those properties. At the edge of the airfield was a ragged line of trees and brush. Could I—just maybe—get over that? Another random memory bubbled up, this one from an article in *Soaring* magazine: to hop a fence at the last minute of a flight, lower the nose to pick up just enough speed to rise over the fence, then dump the glider in on the other side. I had very little altitude to spend, but I did lower the nose, peripherally aware of the mobile home roofs passing just below me, directly aware that even with a little rise I was not going to make it over the tree line. I was not even going to make it to the tops of the trees, where I might try to set the glider down softly.

In the last seconds, amazingly, another random airplane magazine memory surfaced: to land a power plane in trees, pick two trees wider apart then the fuselage of the airplane, but closer together than the wingspan. Go right between them. The wings will sheer off, absorbing much of the airplane's energy and leaving the gasoline in the wing tanks behind.

About all I could do at that point was to pick a pair of trees to hit, but with a last stab at the rudder pedals I picked two moderately tall, stout trees and aimed the nose of the glider right between them. There was a jolt that threw me forward against the seat belts, the glider pitched down and fell briefly.

Then all was still.

I just sat there for a moment. I was alive; that was one thing. I was not in great pain; that was another. I took stock, in a very unsystematic way. The fuselage of the glider was intact, pointed down about 45 degrees, cushioned from the ground by heavy brush. My hat and dark glasses had departed from my head, but were visible just past the instrument console, where the radio and transponder were still on. I reached to turn off the master switch. The canopy lay in the brush beyond the glider's nose, the frame intact, the plexiglass a spider web of cracks, except for a hole about where my head would have hit. The wings stretched out on both sides, buried in the brush.

There was blood on my t-shirt and shorts. Looking for the source, I found a deep gash under my left forearm from wrist to elbow, but it wasn't bleeding much. I didn't take time to be grateful for this, though I did note the lack of pain, and thought I probably had some grace period before the pain hit. I wondered about shock, but put that from my mind. I had to get out of the glider, out of the brush, back to Libby, and to an emergency room. Poor Libby. She must have seen the glider disappear behind the trees. I was sure she must be frantic.

The next 15 minutes were bad.

I was between two fences—the airport's peripheral fence and the mobile home sales-yard fence. Both had barbed wire at the top. I couldn't get over either. To the left and the right were dense brush, mostly blackberry canes, fully thorned and intertwined. I didn't see any poison ivy, but I was sure that must have been mixed in. Taking having survived the crash for granted, I visualized a real dermatological mess in getting back to the airport. Surely the mobile home yard fence stopped somewhere, but I wasn't sure which direction was better.

The only saving grace was the parachute, which I was still wearing. I picked a direction and pushed off into the brush, ducking and backing, using the parachute as a partial shield. I felt thorns raking the skin of my legs and arms, but I didn't stop.

The brush ended more quickly than I expected and I found myself in someone's back yard. At least I knew then the direction of the rear entrance of the airport, and I set off down a neighborhood street, wondering again about shock. My arm had mostly stopped bleeding, though the gash was awful to look at. Would I start to shiver? Would I suddenly get faint? I was probably a mile from the airport entrance. Should I go knock on someone's door and ask them to call 911? I didn't feel all that bad, and I hated to start the train of events that would ensue from a 911 call. Maybe I should try to flag down a passing car?

As I was trying to decide, a car did approach, so I put up my hand. The woman driver of the car waved back and continued past me. I thought of how I must look: blood on my shirt and shorts, disheveled hair, red parachute on my back. I wouldn't have stopped either. But probably, from her distance, she didn't realize anything was wrong.

It was certainly a relief to get to the rear entrance to the airport. I was pretty sure by this time I wasn't going to go into shock. My arm had entirely stopped bleeding. I entered the combination of the gate lock into the keypad, grateful as the gate opened. Looking out across the airport, I saw Libby still standing on the ramp. Maybe she hadn't seen the glider go in. How long had the flight been, anyway? I was sorry she would have to see me walking across the asphalt.

But I had made it.

The rest of the day was anticlimactic. Lib drove us to the London hospital's emergency room, and I entered into their protocols. Everyone seemed amazed that I had walked away from an airplane crash. I heard "You are sure lucky" more times than I could count. I wasn't sure about how I felt, but "lucky" was not at the top of my list.

The hospital people were entirely professional, testing me for everything that could have gone wrong as a result of an airplane crash. But there was only the deep gash. I thought it must have come from the wheel retract lever, which was in about the right place on the left side of the cockpit. That's what I told the surgeon who was to clean the wound and stitch up the multiple layers of tissue that had been torn. He wrote with a magic marker "Yes" on the injured arm, and "No" on the other. I never found out if he was following a careful medical protocol, or just being silly for my benefit.

The End of Soaring

"This is the end of soaring for me."

These were my first words to Libby on the ramp, as I walked up to her in my blood and misery.

That was certainly the way I felt. I was overwhelmed in that moment with the sum of what I had given to be an active soaring pilot—given in training, in licensure, in cash, stress, and time. With the Silent that very morning on my first flight, I had felt that close to it's all having been worth it. To have it brought to nothing by what I saw just then as a chain of bad decisions arising from a minor preventable error…well, it felt as though there was a major imbalance in the order of things. I didn't want to participate in that imbalance anymore.

Libby, wise woman, said, "We'll talk about that later."

Nine years later, I still didn't know how I felt, despite a lot of water under the bridge. My attitude development started on the evening of the crash, when we were contacted by Laurel County's Emergency Management Director. He told us he would watch over the glider—literally watch it through the night from his official SUV—until it could be pulled from the brush and secured. He couldn't have been more concerned or just plain nice. Neither could the representatives from the FAA, the NTSB—the National Transportation Safety Board, to which all accidents had to be reported—or the insurance company with whom I had to deal. All these folks strengthened my sense that I really had been lucky to survive—much less walk away from—a serious airplane crash. They collected the data they needed—personal and aircraft log books, registration, narrative accounts—with impeccable professionalism and genuine caring. I was made to feel a valued member of the flying community. That was precious, and therapeutic.

I spent a fair amount of time going over the flight in my head. Should I have taken more time with the canopy latch on the ground? Joachim Schneibel had demonstrated a test of the latching that was part of his personal checklist: seated and strapped in, after locking the latches, he pushed up on the canopy over his head with his palm. If the canopy were not secure, this push should show it. I had not put that test on my own checklist, convinced that a visual check of the canopy seating was sufficient. Would such a push have indicated an unseated latch?

Given that the latch stayed put through bumpy taxiing from the ramp to the taxiway, more bumps down the taxiway to the runway, and the vibration of a full-throttle takeoff, how could it not have been secure? Why did it release, when it finally did, in smooth, straight-line climbing flight? The NTSB actually sent a representative to Leo Benetti-Longhini's operation in Tullahoma to look at the latching mechanism on an intact Silent. The NTSB guy and Leo together could not figure out how the latch could have released.

I certainly didn't know.

I was equally uncertain about what I had done after the canopy latch did release. Once the canopy's right side lifted up and I had no hope of re-seating it, should I have just let the canopy go? All the questions I had asked in the real time of the flight came back. What if the released canopy had gone into the spinning propeller? I had stopped the engine almost immediately, but what if the canopy had gone into the stopped engine? Worst, I thought, was if the canopy had bounced off and damaged the rudder-elevator assembly. If I had lost rudder and elevator control, the outcome would almost certainly have been horrendous.

Even if the canopy departed with no problem, what would the slipstream in the cockpit have been like with it gone? I had my own experiences in the training glider at Bermuda High as an indication, though the canopy didn't fully release there. And I had read accounts of pilots whose aircraft were struck by birds, birds that came right through the windshield. The onslaught of a sudden, monstrous headwind played havoc with the whole cockpit. I was only flying about 60 mph in the Silent, but even that much direct wind would likely have torn my sunglasses off my face and my hat off my head. I wear large, hard contact lenses, not the small, flexible ones I wore when I was a student pilot at Bermuda High. Without eye protection, would I have even been able to see?

I probably could have stayed above the airport if I had given that the highest priority. But would landing on asphalt have been the best choice? If I had botched the landing—either because of a damaged rudder or elevator, or because I couldn't see, or because of other difficulties in controlling the glider—the asphalt would have been unforgiving. The infield between the runway and taxiways was grass, but the surface below the grass was irregular, full of ridges and potholes. The airport manager had told me never to try to land the glider on the grass. I would have gone for the asphalt.

Right after the crash I was convinced that almost the worst of all outcomes had come to pass, partly because of my incompetence, and partly because of uncontrollable circumstances. But the more I thought about it and replayed the sequence of events, the more I came to wonder if actually the best outcome hadn't transpired. Once the canopy latch released, the flight was doomed. Almost every other way I played it, the outcome was worse than what had actually happened. I had actually done a pretty good job of damage control.

I waffle about this conclusion, but at least, nine years later, it is a viable emotional stance for me.

Other folks helped me deal with my loss in ways they saw fitting. I was contacted by a Silent owner in Tennessee who had been thinking of selling a glider exactly like mine (but newer) and might be willing to pass it on to me at a substantial discount. Leo offered to help me obtain one of the new electrically-powered Silents from Italy at a reduced price through creative shipping. My insurance company announced their willingness to insure me in another glider.

But I was not ready for ownership again.

What stopped me as much as anything was the vision given to me by my few weeks of putting flying the glider first in my life. It was a tremendous commitment. It was not something I could do occasionally, once a week, maybe for an hour, like I flew the Cessna. Being an active soaring pilot meant that I would have to make flying the glider the default activity for most of my spare time. Driving to London, preparing the glider, flying, cleaning it and putting it up, driving home—that would be a whole day's activity. And I would have to devote most of the flyable days between May and October to just that. My wife and I have complicated lives. We are both active writing professionals. We have children and grandchildren in distant states, people whose lives we want to be part of. We devote a portion of almost every day to physical activity. Was I prepared to re-prioritize my whole life to put flying the glider at the top of that list?

I didn't think so.

I have thought about the commitment of the other members of the soaring club I was a member of for two years. Four out of five Saturdays and Sundays from April to November found the core club members at the airfield, pretty much all day. If they weren't flying, they were assisting on the flight line, doing glider maintenance, or towing. They were at the airfield even when conditions were unflyable, just for the fellowship, just to be around others with the same interest. I didn't feel that way. There were too many other things to do on lovely summer weekends.

Sometimes I felt as if my crash had culminated in a kind of revelation. I was just not going to be able to be an active, independent soaring pilot. Making that decision after my one glorious flight that morning with the Silent would have been difficult. After the crash, it was a much easier decision to make.

This did not mean I gave up soaring altogether. Our older son lives near Minneapolis. Forty miles south of him, a commercial soaring operation thrives on the airport in Faribault. Don Ingraham is the proprietor, flight instructor, and chief pilot. A friendlier and more enthusiastic proponent of soaring would be hard to imagine. In 2017, in the April after the crash, I booked some hours with Don in his high-performance, two-place German sailplane, and I had a very good time indeed. For the initial flights I let Don do the high-precision parts—the take-offs and landings—while I flew in the clean, open air. We soared with a pair of bald eagles and with a migrating flock of white pelicans. We made some tentative cross-country forays, reading clouds and gauging thermal-producing landscapes. We gaggled with another circling glider, watching the sun flash off its freshly-polished wings. It was fine flying. I made another reservation for August, when next we would go up to visit our son.

Until the pandemic in 2020, when travel of all sorts was shut down, this was the extent of my soaring—twice a year with Don Ingraham. Soaring was good to look forward to, but it didn't take over my life. It didn't even take over my flying life. I still flew the Cessna, watching from the air as the seasons turned in the agricultural fields and forested knobs here in Kentucky. I flew with Libby, letting her open the passenger window in the cockpit to make photographs of the crisscrossed fields beneath us, or with friends, or just sightseeing by myself. Not very many people get to do even this. I was fortunate to have the privilege.

Yet…there is undeniably a tinge of yearning left, and with it a kind of resistance to the conclusion that my flying life had to come out this way. I found myself looking back to the various junctures, thinking, What could I have done differently? and searching for some kind of life lesson to take away from the choices I made.

The juncture I come back to most often is associated with the Chilhowee Gliderport in Tennessee, where in five action-packed days in 2003, under the tutelage of Sarah Kelly Arnold, I added aerotow sailplane privileges to my private flying certificate. I have written about this briefly in Chapter 8, "Belonging." But there is more to the story.

I was pretty pumped by the end of my time at Chilhowee. I had successfully flown a two-place training glider in decidedly gusty conditions: eight successive solo aerotows and landings on my second-to-last day there. I had survived a minor emergency—a low-altitude loss of engine power by the tow plane—by releasing and landing straight ahead to the tow-plane's right, just as all the books say to do. I had executed a masterful check ride with a notoriously idiosyncratic pilot examiner. I was comfortable and confident in the training glider, and eager to move up to the next level of performance.

The stable of gliders for rent at Chilhowee included a higher-performance single-place wood-and-fabric glider and, as luck would have it, a non-self-launching, pure-glider Silent 2.

I had noticed the Silent when it was first imported into the U.S. It was smaller than the standard "high-performance" gliders from Germany and Eastern Europe, but higher performance than many of them, all composite of course, with ample use of carbon fiber. It was the only Italian glider on the American market, and, at least at first, was less expensive than the equivalently-performing gliders. It was exciting for me to think of getting to fly one. I asked Sarah what would be required for me to be allowed to fly it. She said I would have to fly the older single-place glider enough to be comfortable with it before she would check me out in the Silent, maybe half a dozen flights.

I was excited enough for Libby and me to stay an extra day at Chilhowee so I could try the single-place glider.

I remember the cockpit being quite tight, almost claustrophobic when I first wriggled in, with an upright seating position. But the glider handled beautifully on tow, so much lighter and more responsive than the trainer. I had quite a thrilling two-hour flight along the ridge adjoining the airfield, arcing back and forth ten miles each way, buoyed up by the wind over the slope. I emerged from the flight full of vows to come back and earn my way into the Silent.

My enthusiasm was dampened just before Libby and I left by a random conversation I had sitting on the porch of the operations trailer. I and another observer whom I did not know were watching a pilot in the Silent execute a series of take-offs and landings. It was a beautiful sailplane to watch. I commented that it was an extremely capable glider, and the price for the self-launching version was notably less than for equivalent gliders.

"I don't know about that," the other observer said. "Have you looked at the price for a new one lately?"

I said I had not, actually. But the last time I had looked it had been in the $80,000 range.

"Oh, no," the other observer said. "Depending on the trailer and all, it'll be well into the 120s now. And you never see a used one."

Mid 120s? I remember being instantly, palpably deflated. I realized that I had been spinning a fantasy a little below my conscious level. I would master the old single place glider at Chilhowee, then, with Sarah's careful help, transition to the Silent. With sufficient time (and rental fees) I would master the Silent. Then—somehow—a self-launching Silent would become available to me. But mid-120s. That was more than used, performance-comparable, self-launching German gliders were advertised for. It was a range of cost for a glider that I had never planned to explore.

When Libby and I got home I checked current pricing on the Alisport website and found that my porch conversant had been right. A potential purchaser had to be prepared to pay in the mid-120's for a self-launching Silent 2, probably more. I experienced more deflation. No fantasy could support that kind of price. In a market with no used gliders, I was just an outsider. What would be the point of my getting checked out for the rental Silent at Chilhowee if there was never to be the possibility of my flying one, except by coming back there?

I banished thoughts of a Silent from the realm of possibility. And I never went back to the Chilhowee Gliderport.

That is a juncture at which I might have done things differently. Two things, in fact.

The first is just to have pursued my enthusiasm and gone back to Chilhowee to learn to fly the Silent. My glider flying skills were freshly polished by my activities there. My capacities were current. I had momentum. If I had progressed through the older, single place glider into the state-of-the-art Silent, I would have had the experience of flying a modern, high performance glider three years before the second, self-launching Silent appeared on my horizon. When it did appear, I would have been a more knowledgeable purchaser and flown it better, more comfortably, in the early days of my ownership.

The second thing I might have done was right after the crash, when Leo Benetti offered to sell me a new electric Silent. I told him no. I could have told him I was in the market for a used, self-launching Silent. There were about 12 Silents in the country back in 2016 and Leo knew everything that was going on with all of them. If someone were thinking of selling one, Leo would have known about it. Perhaps an announced buyer would have motivated someone to sell. But one way or another, Leo's knowledge would have been an asset to me.

As far as life lessons…the only thing I can think of is pretty trite and unhelpful, but it is heartfelt. Go for it. Or, as Nike ad men have it, Just Do It. If you are sure you want some experience—and it survives tests of not harming others or the planet—go for it. If you wait for the perfect set of circumstances to conjoin, or for some extraordinary event to transpire, you are likely not to realize the experience. Our lives, particularly our physically- and mentally-capable lives, are finite. As soon as your best-judgment says you can, go for your desired experience. Bludgeon your way forward if you have too. But narrow your eyes to focus on the key component and go straight ahead.

I think I spent too much time waiting for the perfect set of circumstances in my search for the kind of flying I wanted to do. I should have been a little more hard-eyed and admitted to myself fairly close to the beginning of my adventures at Bermuda High that only a self-launching sailplane was going to give me the kind of experience I wanted.

But though the road might have been different if I had admitted that and proceeded accordingly, I don't think the end point would have been any different. As I said before, being an active soaring pilot, even with a self-launching sailplane, means that I would have to fly the glider every time the weather permitted it. I was not willing to do that early on, with the demands and joys of family and work, and I am not willing to do that now.

Just not willing.

If there is a tinge of yearning still left, well…. Life is a complicated and multi-layered enterprise.

Soaring for me will always be one of the layers.

Out of the Air

Little did Libby and I know when we saw our first sailplane in the middle of a field in Germany in 1967 what a complicated journey we would have in aviation. We couldn't know how many ups and downs we would face in my realizing my newly-reawakened longing to fly in general, and to soar in particular. We couldn't have foreseen the peak experiences and the frustrations, the personalities and idiosyncrasies of those who led us on this journey. And we couldn't possibly have imagined what patience and fortitude the journey would require of me, and the reserves I would draw on in order to get as far as I did into flying.

In the category of peak experiences I first count my running hooked to a hang glider at the Lookout Mountain Flight Park (described in Chapter 6, "The Hills"). The feeling of really flying as my legs left the ground was purely ecstatic. Every other aspect of the scene—the presence of my companions on the hill, the wind, the scruffy hang glider—all disappeared in the momentary magic of actually flying.

I count too as a peak my soloing Lucian Bartosik's trike at the end of a long five days of struggling. (See my account in Chapter 7, "Trikes.") The feeling of mastery I experienced, of the union of me and the machine, a union in flying, was enveloping. I felt after those flights as if I could conquer the world. I certainly count my "perfect flight" in the Silent sailplane (described in the first chapter, "Perfect Flight") as a third peak experience of my flying career, perhaps the most profound of all. Coming after a variety of frustrations, the experience of all the airplane's systems coming together in perfect harmony filled me with a kind of ecstasy different from what I felt at Lookout Mountain, but no less fulfilling. For that moment, and for the other peak moments, I was supremely happy. I asked nothing more out of life.

Of course each of the peak experiences had its downside too. The downsides of soloing Lucian's trike and flying the Silent occurred right after the peaks, creating the two greatest attitude swings of my life. The downside of my experience with hang gliders was more protracted. But in all three cases, what seemed like a golden opportunity was obliterated by circumstances.

As well, my interest in flying has led to some fine—though not peak—experiences, experiences that developed over time, and came with enough structure to lack the sharpness of the peaks. Besides Libby's and my first glimpse of a sailplane in 1967, I think of the latter days at Bermuda High and my first flight in a German fiberglass glider there, of my experiences on the ridge at Chilhowee, of the latter days of my flying Lucian's trike, of my seeing the ad for the Silent in the Wings and Wheels classifieds and talking about it with Libby.

Finally, I think of returning to KRGA, my Madison County home airport, in the Cessna 150 after various flights, the late afternoon air silky and smooth. I may have been returning after a flight north to Reed Valley Orchard in Paris, or south to the airport in London, east across the Owsley Fork Reservoir to Irvine, or west to the Abbey of Gethsemani and on past it to Bardstown. All these flights share senses of comfort, but also of participation in an experience beyond the everyday, of an unusual opportunity taken advantage of. They involve the melding of my skillset with the physical environment, an "I actually did this" feeling to go with the steady throbbing of the engine, the constantly changing view over the struts, the scans of the instruments and the intermittent radio calls.

It was a lovely feeling to have.

In spite of the depths of feelings like this, on Friday, March 9, 2023, I sold the Cessna.

One reason was the condition of my eyes. Cataract surgery in 2021 resulted in reduced visual acuity in my right eye. I was in danger of losing my flying privileges at my next FAA physical exam. I would still be able to apply for a Certificate of Demonstrated Ability, but getting that was a long shot.

Besides, the airport had gotten crowded. The ever-growing Eastern Kentucky University Aviation Studies program (the only baccalaureate Aviation Studies program in the state of Kentucky) made thorough use of the airspace around the airport, with some 30 airplanes, over 300 students, and more than 45,000 take-offs and landings a year. That congestion had begun to make my flying difficult, sometimes even unpleasant.

A third reason why I sold the Cessna: I had a really good prospective buyer, Shannon Mathis.

Shannon was then the Director of Maintenance for the whole airport (KRGA). He was responsible to Eastern Kentucky University for all its airplanes. Every one of these airplanes had to be gone over thoroughly every 100 flight hours, by mandate of the FAA. I myself had depended on Shannon's operation to perform my own FAA-mandated Annual Inspection on the 150. Shannon directed a staff of FAA-certified mechanics to carry out these periodic inspections and do general maintenance on the airplanes of some of the airport's general aviation denizens. He and his mechanics knew a lot about Cessnas.

A master of things mechanical—he maintained a lovely Harley-Davidson motorcycle which he rode to the airport on nice days—Shannon did not have a pilot's license. I had named him as a Designated Insured on the 150's insurance policy for 2022-23, and he had been doing some short training flights with the EKU Chief Instructor, a friend of his. When I decided to sell my airplane to him, I was sure he would use it to get his license. He would be the fifth person, including me, to get his license in that airplane under my ownership.

Shannon would make a good owner of the 150. He would maintain the airplane well, flying it regularly, re-doing the interior, planning ultimately to repaint the whole airplane. (He had a friend who ran a motorcycle paint shop.)

"If you ever want to sell this plane, I want to buy it," Shannon had said, after the first maintenance he did on the 150. He stood by that pronouncement. He and I settled on a price. The Airport Manager said, "The hangar goes with the airplane." So Shannon took over the 150, in the hangar I had occupied for ten years, the one the previous owner had occupied before that.

My formal relation with the airport and with flying was severed.

Well…almost. I do retain my membership in the Soaring Society of America, the Experimental Aircraft Association, and the U.S. Hang Glider and Paraglider Association, more for old time's sake and a desire to support these organizations than for involvement in activities. I have an interest in the Aircraft Owners and Pilots Association (AOPA), which sends me a glossy magazine every month and keeps me up-to-date on issues the aviation community cares about. The local EAA chapter meets periodically and sponsors Young Eagles Rallys, in which young people ages 8-18 are flown free of charge by general aviation and EKU pilots. I no longer schedule my life around these opportunities, but Libby and I participate when we can.

And there is Condor. In bursts of interest I fly a glider over Slovenia and sightsee, keeping up my flying skills. Condor is a remarkable instrument, and I should take more advantage of it than I do. But I am satisfied to operate at the level I have worked out.

I still care about airplanes, though as Libby and I and our grandchildren age we find ourselves on commercial aviation at 35,000 feet more often than low and slow in small planes. This trend will likely increase. I no longer fantasize about being up among the cumulus clouds on summer days. I no longer dream about flying. That world has receded into the background of Libby's and my lives.

In writing about this aspect of my life, I have tried to understand for myself both where my fixation with flying and airplanes came from (the second and third chapters here) and how it worked itself out (all the rest of the book).

I do not miss the outlays associated with owning an airplane—the hangar fees, the insurance premiums, the medical expenses, the inevitable maintenance costs, even the expense of the 100-octane, low-lead gasoline I fed the 150's engine. And I know that at this stage of our lives, Libby and I must be starting to pare down our possessions and commitments. An airplane is certainly a possession that comes with its share of commitments. I'm glad I can feel happy about where my plane has ended up.

But I do miss the flights in the late afternoon air. I miss the "discovery" flights I offered to my friends, most of whom had never flown in a light airplane before, never seen their dwellings and the ground-based sights so familiar to them from an elevation 2000 feet above the ground.

I miss the wonder in their voices as they take in my airplane ownership: "You own an airplane?!"

"I used to," I have to say now.

"But I don't anymore."

About the Author

About the Author

Roger Jones is a historian of science who has long been fascinated by the way creatures move through the air. In addition to academic writing, he has published short stories involving flight and nonfiction pieces in flying magazines. He is the author of *The Mists of Arltunga*, a novel set in the Australian Outback between the two world wars, and *Victor T. Vulture*, a coming-of-age novella about a vegetarian buzzard. A member of Bluegrass Writers Studio (Eastern Kentucky University), Berea Writers Circle, and Northfield Open Writers, he is working on a short story collection based on songs by Canadian musician Stan Rogers and a collection of essays on alternative means of flight. He lives in Berea, KY, with his wife, Libby, also a writer. For more, see https://www.rogerjoneswriter.net

Gil, Rafe, Roger, and Libby Jones with Roger's Cessna 150, 2005

www.ingramcontent.com/pod-product-compliance
Lightning Source LLC
LaVergne TN
LVHW010836120826
845149LV00017B/1474